JUMP
THE
CLOCK

JUMP THE CLOCK

NEW & SELECTED POEMS

ERICA HUNT

NIGHTBOAT BOOKS

NEW YORK

ISBN: 978-1-64362-024-4

Cover Art: Carmen Herrera, *Iberic*, 1949. Acrylic on canvas on board; 40 inches. The Metropolitan Museum of Art, Gift of Tony Bechara, in celebration of the Museum's 150th Anniversary, 2019. © Carmen Herrera. Courtesy of the artist and Lisson Gallery.

Interior Art: Woodcuts by Alison Saar from *Arcade*, 1996, appear on pages 22, 80 and 100. © Alison Saar. Courtesy of the artist. All other interior images courtesy of Erica Hunt.

Design and typesetting by adam b. bohannon
Text set in Gotham and Sabon

Cataloging-in-publication data is available from the Library of Congress

Nightboat Books
New York
www.nightboat.org

CONTENTS

VERONICA: A SUITE IN X PARTS

Local History

Preface

I was thinking that if the ceiling were mirrored we would have
to watch what we say about what we feel. That we could not use
curtains to conceal what we know. That we could watch without
leaving the room or the chair. We could watch the sun take over or
the sun pulled up short. Watch the hard stream of current events
proceed in yanks or lurches.

We could eliminate the ritual of walking around ourselves, meet
head on, relying on how pure coincidence transforms trial and error.
No more being thrown off beat.

It must be love if while beside you I think of you and don't fall in.

I could throw away my hat, I need the target practice.

We could get down to work. Work as the metaphor for the idea we
can touch: fingers and thumb putting matter into fact, and cease
being Sunday Sandinistas.

We could argue, get sprained on topic mountain and pass the whole
night putting our shoulders to the planet.

We could remove the calvinist and other secret furniture from the
language.

Except when the power cuts out, and being comes off as paint.
Except when we are nobody's and I'm the only one left to catch me.

Except when the calm we've kept comes off in conversation and
they've beaten the last stranger who wandered into their midst.

Or when the bricks of the aircraft we're flying in begin to migrate slowly apart far from the finish line.

Except when the exits aren't marked and the busses have stopped running at this hour.

When we believe we have no other choice but to run while motionless.

Until we stop waiting for solutions from afar that will never be given. Until balance is fulfilled by the barely contiguous unfamiliar. Until the texture of rain is wet with visible points. Until the decay in language doesn't fix logic.

Until we enlist sense to illumination and make room for the blanks.

In the Corner of the Eye

She must be someone's missing person, the unread portion. She
sits on the stoop tearing pages out of 18-month-old Penthouse
magazines that someone has stacked for recycling. The gray sky is an
emulsion of humidity and promised rain. She's oblivious beneath her
umbrella eating french toast and a large orange juice that someone
walked out without paying for.

She is a victim of a conspiracy of her teeth that keeps her away from
the food she loves, raw carrots, com, apples, raisins. She is *forced*
to order omelettes and french toast. Sometimes she offers to sweep
the floors, rinse the windows of their daily ashes and to defer to the
empty plate that poverty and the times demand. It depends. When
it's busy, her strategies are good currency, the currency of good will.

She's wearing a skirt and pants and it's cold and she's between sexes
just now. She's wearing shoes that don't fit her feet, like old felt hats
at the ends of her legs.

One of the definitions of being a person is that another person is
talking to you. The person is particular, unlike that diffuse group of
people you don't spend time with who are all pronouns. This person
is the source of certain facts but not the facts that she ever speaks
out loud. This person you become accustomed to: her buckle, our
buckle, her pins, our pins, her ankles, our ankles, her limp, our limp.
Your person or her person, it doesn't matter across the line of the
middle ground.

A Coronary Artist

I dream excess—high-speed vision. Snow falling upwards. The bed in a corner of the empty lot. Cut logs careening away from the saw. (They know what's waiting for them.) A line of introductions. An incomplete arc of contemplation.

A family of clothes beg to be picked up. Chimneys at work carry steam. Ingest coffee; loosen stuck bits of flux loved for their silence.

All the great heroes slept late. The common folks get up early and fight for the victory. It takes a lifetime to be steered in this direction; snow is mounting from the sky down. I think the dirty clothes are crying and want to be washed. Piles of clothes begin to mount from the sky down. I would say no, except for the empty chair, where taking off is perfected.

The left brain turns the other cheek. The right brain can't imagine it. To be bringing one's face into morning when it's barely light. To promote sunshine to my daughter while surviving my own ferocious will to sleep. This is the comer to tum to the bathroom. This is the sink, I look at myself in the mirror and see the person I might have been had I gotten more sleep. I step back into the world. It's warmer and moister than I thought. It is a whole world, with its own affections, anxieties, welcome.

Custom has it that a woman gets up first to solve the dilemma of the burning moment.

You can smell the smoke answering the alarm.

And then you can't smell anything over the family soundtrack, putting everything on hold. One becomes an adult without knowing the details of how it was done, knowing only which team you're on, which hat corresponds to your glands.

Already this is an extinct culture, a culture of giants prone to the vertigo of silent agreements and unenforceable contracts. The rocks in our beds belong to them. Their sexual politics get the better of us sometimes and we are left with dream transcriptions and delinquencies instead of passion outside the parentheses.

We make it to the crossroads only to come to a stop. The idea we harbor is subversive. That there may be many moments in which we recognize the sources of our hunger, falling out of the sky, a complete thought sung to our most visible selves.

The Order of the Story

I

Imagine yourself walking into a room the exercise suggests, and then, describe how you fill the doorway, the direction you dress in, the way you walk out of the frame. Imagine finding stones—the inscriptions that predicted you.

Invent the language now. Invent the language as if each inflection belonged to you instead of containing you, or treating you as if you were a commotion in the path of progress.

Invent a language to describe the doorway in the person. Eyes growing accustomed to the dark, till the dark has layers peeling off in shiny blue slices. Here and there flashes as the tongue licks over the heart.

Describe the figure the doorway supports. Into this trope come declensions, all the detail her mortal frame can claim, stick and join. Where the mind's orbit has faded into thoughts disguised as recalculation, where she shows signs of adjustment: a walking chainsaw in crinoline and spandex, a smile outlined by name.

Describe where the heart goes in and out of her, where the exits are marked. Indicate which team she's on, the team of Moms, for the love of them, however the bread gets sliced.

Describe the buts in the doorway, in the doorway and everywhere in between, where she trips or slides down them into some other contingency, a sentence with a dangling clause.

She is the figure in the vicinity of her experience with its distracting claims on her attention. Capital letters inflate routine, without which days curve away.

Describe an exile where the landscape is mute. Muffled under plexiglass beneath a ball that does not drop.

A person in the doorway who feels the pull of the earth, a mighty planet, third from the sun.

Where small talk is offered as evidence that one fits some place. Where the characters have names, open-and-shut cases of assumed identity, and hold down their spots in a book.

Where the characters read the book as they are writing it, form and informant. In this book the withered see with their own eyes, and are therefore plump and spry. The young imagine a future flat and limitless amidst insurable and calculated risks, in which time is a lake, and the reflection of one's face stares up to the sky behind her. Each face is personal, each figure of safety, of love is particular.

Gloss
(a catalog of feeling)

approach:
to find one's tongue in one's mouth.
courtship:
to use an assumed name.
romance:
to pencil the present, to pack
the brackets, to sightread weather.
request:
to test the heat for empty;
to talk straight.
refusal:
to walk around oneself.
denial:
to have the last word.
flirt:
she writes a text backwards to a curtained modesty.
appeasement:
he paints himself in.
passion:
adjectives wag the dog.
passion:
she takes a step back and can see herself fully in a darkened pane of
glass in the kitchen window.
passion:
he thought sentences had only two sides to them, bottom and top;
now love multiplies possible positions.
hard:
he throws his gravelly voice, shifts from where he begins and ends.
pursuit of motion:
she breaks into present tense,

<u>she</u> spins through her skin,

<u>she</u> shows her muscle.

erase of borders:

<u>she</u> drinks, draining the cup, thinks it's the same one she poured.

stepping off:

<u>he</u> is impatient to be that one with her.

stepping off:

<u>her</u> subplot as well, their armor looks related.

immersion:

they lock eyes and are surprised by the vertigo.

he puts his thumbs in his ears and hears his heart un-ribboning,

sound and rhythm in the distance.

she feels like paper caught in the updraft of a quiet explosion.

Who lit the match? The lights flicker, and it spreads, every

conversation ending with a question.

practice:

the day to day gives her an edge to stand on;

how the calendar divides;

fine grains defeat the measure, nor do others fit our preset

containers.

They are to each other the humblest examples of the chase elsewhere

meaning the feeling out of the corner of the eye.

practice:

novelty repeats the new: to even speak the name she listens.

chance:

she opens the door ready not to know who she will meet next.

The Order of the Story

II

She opens the door. He is standing there with such complete attention she turns to see who could be standing in the door just over her shoulder. She doesn't know whether to smile, whether this will send the wrong message. She smiles at him, she wants to close the door. She opens the door.

She comes to the doorway. She is nothing like he thought she would be, shy in her own house. Her head is to one side, uncombed, unruly spirals, but otherwise dressed and ready. He wants to say something to her.

He wants to ask her whose side she is on in the total war - the one without a name—**which side protects her**—in the exchange of bullets. Friendly or indiscriminate, the echo carves air around him, the fire's trapped in scar-stretched skin, the hole gunfire left is large enough to fill a room with grief, the doors locked behind him.

Time fore ... all of a sudden ... shortened, he wants back *into* this: restful periods of reasonable expectation, events with commas, the supple ease of free association. He wants *out of* the line of fire, he wants back into the ground taken from him in a chain of mistaken events:

a thief mistakes him for a thief or a neighbor mistakes him for a housebreaker. A cop with the power of gun mistakes him for a perp out of line. He wants out of the extreme.

Clearly he wants to say something to her. She watches him, the traffic of emotion on his face becoming light or extinct one after the other. She opens the door wider, as if to say come in.

He watches her face rise into focus. The balloons float out of the frame of the doorway, carrying her lines, her walk-on scene stage instructions. He watches this knowing there is more than one scenario, more than one way to connect the dots, more than one ending.

He closes his eyes to imagine it frankly, un-retouched—an image of safety, his own body flat moving along the camouflage of trees.

Local History
(cold war breaks)

the planet in the song
the planet in the song
which planet do you mean?
The planet in the song.

I

X number of persons are manufactured in this country every minute. When I finished this sentence there were two more. We are completely unknown to each other so keep a respectful distance. It takes a wrap-around imagination, to separate our lives from the statistics. Look, I'm beside myself. The spotlight is moving in a slow arc in time to the music. Our figures jump, cast model shadows on the screen. Which one am I?

A person in history, we don't know what that means; we have only the social remains, a current preoccupation. A person in history is a person from the past. Someone answers an ad based on a description of the dream body for a modest fee. The tombstones continue the shell game under a parsed identity.

A person looking back sees a long stretch of things to remember. Important people who have died of proximate causes. The seven billion people living now are descended from a handful of common folk who lived on the books. Each day they scaled the dull edge of routine, to shower, write, dress, look after the kids long enough to kiss good morning, go to work, come home so that we may live a life they never imagined in which we shower, write, dress, look after the kids, go to work and come home.

A certain amount can be predicted from the past, I'm told. Power centers run off excess, wipe small towns off the map.

The townspeople of Double Park, for instance, drink well water that makes them ill. Their elected officials arrange public meetings as alibis: to execute smiles and thank their critics.

Work is overcoming resistance, to push past the sense that there's nothing left to do, it's all been written before, falling off the inventory shelves.

Even if the narrator could be trusted what keeps the reader from calling the shots? Many of the names I read about in the history books I had never heard spoken aloud, so I put them in a separate place in my head, hung with a do-not-disturb sign. I had every ambition to read the book to the end, even if I had to write it. But I know how it all turns out—the 20th century.

For the movie version, which soon will be the only version anyone remembers, they will employ a cast of several hundred. Leaving out the war scenes for the moment, many of the century's towering moments will entail a stunning deployment of the industry's greatest effects.

A dozen artificial suns will be required, each with its own shade of light. The designer will use thousands of cans of spray dirt carefully dyed to match the movie's changing terrain. Three of the world's largest cities will block off their streets for a month to accommodate shooting. Cars will be rebuilt and repainted 16 separate times to be used in separate chase scenes. An all-star cast as well as a crew of distinguished screenplay writers will be required. A whole new category of police will have to be invented. The longest movie ever made. People will go to see it in order to be alone.

For the war scenes they will employ smoke machines so that the battlefield will float towards the audience. The noise of the artillery will emanate from both behind and directly in front of the viewer to re-enforce the urge to duck for cover. The war will be shot from a perspective that even its veterans never experienced high in their planes, far away studying their gridded screens. Corpses will jump with the impact of automatic gunfire, the bushes will bend -maybe even combust as if really in the vicinity of guerrilla fighting in Natal, Compton, East New York. The background will be scored for a 24-hour talk-radio format: a woman's voice reading the news, the names of casualties, cleansers and aerosols without affect. The air breaking down into its component parts, heavy with the odor of spoiling flesh.

Routine explanations of atrocity will be clocked, to present them precisely as they do on the evening news. Anchors will play themselves; mime a mix of concern and fatigue, as if the news had happened to them. It will be entertaining however. A final shot of the earth, a ball inclined in the air, framed over a permanent beach suspended in a dark blue firmament.

I turn off the conveyor belt. Sooner or later history catches up.

II
Celebrated persons did attend this century of extremes. They hurried out as soon as they did their bit, or else they sat back down and snored during the others' presentations.

I, too, have a feeling that I've been here before. Someone has. There are rows of us, an entire generation between the ages of 25 and 40, though the dates of the nuclear age are to some extent arbitrary. So much of our formative life has evolved in a globe held hostage by bombs, we have grown an exaggerated sense of the present.

We *discovered* youth—a spontaneous and insatiable state of desire, both the proof and engine of a transient prosperity: thus our arguments spring up, we have no memory of tilling up the public square before, uncurling our banners and daring the police to fight or join us.

We have a problem with novelty, we are bound to repeat the new. Plots in which the walls are torn down with our bare hands, the sense that an immense tide of history will sweep realpolitik in a somersault are tamed within frames with blurred captions.

History acquires its perfect specificity in succeeding versions.

City

I

One lives inside the replica of a city materializing from the sum of its inhabitants' aspirations, fluctuating on a dial of pluses and minuses. The replica city commands a momentum separate from the city for which one has bought a ticket. The real city swallows the evidence of your arrival, while in the other, where exemplary forgeries abound, it is difficult to read the intention that launched you here, as the words themselves, now realized, dry in their new positions.

In both cities, members of shifting teams have unspoken tasks tending the myths around landmarks, starting the fires, burdening the wires for the headlines back home.

The exits in public spaces are frequently blocked by a crowd at pains to avoid the question of how many can reasonably fit. One travels at a velocity necessary to see both cities, for half of what is seen one could have dreamt up oneself, and for that latter special half one is anxious to transmit as fearlessly as possible, how good it seems to be here, wish you were here, I remain, etc.

Taste has much to machine down, silly spectacles to explain, monotonies to apportion. Paris was not easily surprised in the last century, nor are we less impatient. At an early age, one is already too late to pick out favorites. It is a little like choosing hormones or which animal shall produce wool.

Nevertheless, life is thought to consist of making such choices and leaving one's stamp on nature. In this first march, one is the master of one's happiness, no matter how it is described. When one ceases to attend to it, one is no longer an intimate collaborator but a footdragger behind an abstract protagonist.

The planetarium, the aquatic park, the botanical garden are parts
of Nature which are known and catalogued, in order to distract the
emotion which desires to know its own location and the location of
others' feelings, no matter how impossible the possession of any degree
of certainty. Irregularities are sequestered for proper observation,
resident in cities of planned unpredictability, where rodents tent in trees
(contrary to the law of habitat), and butterflies burrow, deriving the
stain of their wings like flowers, from the soil. One arrives in the zone
of detachable parts, dangerously soft, ripe for collision.

II

I had been home before to make payments on that genre. But still life is
poor evidence of what those represented objects are when they are not
under observation. Enthusiasm has its own physics; illuminated objects
are its visual echo. The cornices in which I saw at first engraved voice
and grandeur were self-administered, an antidote brought by my eyes
from a previous landscape of surfaces seemingly free from gravity.

We took rooms right off the curb and felt lucky for it, for otherwise
there were no rooms to be had, so divergent was the fanfare of the
city's fame from the means to operate it. Of these rooms we made a
better face and they expanded to accommodate our cargo; the hall
took the length of our ladders, the water reached our closets, the
buckets doubled as pots for plants and caught the leaks.

And then there was sex, whose random episodes we learned were
interdisciplinary and ritually diluted, we turned to study as opposed
to practice. Public conjunctions were rare, though when they
occurred, as when one looks up from a newspaper and notices the
train car is full, the principals remained in character in separate
plays, indifferent to the ordinary scales of appreciation, except to the
universal pursuit of shoes—the more fantastic, the more suggestive
of passionate commute. Too unseasoned to be more than spectators,
we tapped our toes affably.

It was very soon after we arrived, when the city, however plural, we heard as a dialect, as a distinct manner of speaking. We were as startled as if we had heard a stranger using our mother's habits of speech, a turn at once familiar and uncanny, that made us fall into an intimacy with our neighbors, joined by a mother tongue, despite it being a lingua franca of a different era.

Pushed to the utmost of our capacity by the burden of faith and expectation, we collapsed, imitating the habits of the people in our surroundings without knowing their meanings.

We took grease with our coffee regular. We were contrite after feasts of rich food. We gambled, even on hills.

III

The paper and the words printed on them, shredded up by professional blades, had been thrown out in boxes, eeled in the air a spiralling blizzard that wet the sidewalks and gutters just after Christmas and before New Year's which everyone planned to avoid separately.

You know, I don't think anyone teaches you how to glaze the eyes. I think that acting as if you don't see what's in front of you is a matter of taking a walk backwards, mentally, from the person in front of you.

The past tense of read is read.

See.

I mean that you become aware of obscure dynastic differences—the impossibility, for instance, of asking the guy beside you with the aroma of a public shelter but fresh creases in his pants, why he is reading Herodotus upside down.

done already
right side up

One becomes accustomed to thinking within one's own noise.

IV
We found in separate editions an unexpected glut of disasters. It was not possible to read without violence. Certain poisons have the distinction of being palatable in small doses while proving toxic later. The result was wisdom without liberation, risk without lyricism.

This served to compound our primitive fears of the dark, of strangers without money, of strangers with too much money, of large animals, of heights over water, of not having enough money to go out, of arriving too early, of arriving without being noticed, of being too fond of the park, of riding the subway too often, of not enough sunlight and so on and so on wherever ignorance might be disguised as prudence, since it had happened to someone, an infinite supply of them—the multiplication of grotesque loss of life and limb spread like a disease, out of proportion to the population, which no matter how anonymous, was slowly dividing into a *them* and an *us*. The disease of not knowing or seeing for oneself but having it told to you made it more contagious, unchanging virus, and changing in circumstances manufactured completely in the imagination, without enlightenment.

We found substitutes for immersion. A private tone, an abstract public character. Newly appointed our surrogates behaved in all the observances we found distasteful. Thus it was these acquaintances who heard the odd footstep, who held our pocketbooks closer, who glanced behind us on the street, and it was they who lived our outside for us, inside us, just as recently arrived as we ourselves were in a place we made home but which we refused to call by its name.

Household tips

Don't reach for the handle.
Use baking soda, corn-starch or molasses.
A child's wail is the equivalent to a scarlet flamboyant.
Give someone a ride.
Electricity can be generated by a pair of rubber-soled shoes, teeth in
a comb and an acrylic carpet.
In the event of a recent death, face mirrors towards the walls, lest
you see what you didn't want to see when they were alive.
A dead bolt will prevent one's foes from leaving the bathroom.
Open the good liquor then.
Return everything as you found it.
Empty the pockets and don't get hung up on the drama.
Keeping one eye closed will cause the pencil to appear about to roll
off the table upon leaving your hand, and make Mr. S. appear a
complete stranger.
An incriminating stain is best removed.
Your friends will be diplomatic; your silence an accessory.

open door

There are events that I forget, that I don't remember forgetting, that make me uneasy, I so easily surrender them, jammed in a passageway of unacknowledged storage.

Together we pick up the pieces dreams anticipate through texture. Emblems tied together by oblique chains of recall. We work backwards, inventing continuity on the drive to see some thing stunning, something to vary our hunger, something to sustain the stranger within ourselves with indelible landmarks.

He forgets too. We forget to allow for what we have forgotten. I resist maps, he knows the way there, if we don't get lost. We miss a turn because we haven't compensated for the shift of ground when our joint shadows don't yet merge.

We read into the same little girl, our daughter, whose temperament is just emerging, who might be based on something we have forgotten out of focus in our future. All the mythologies have this in common: the transformations, a tree that was once a lovely woman, a stream that echoes laughter, the fluttering foliage marking the track on which a woman must run to own herself, points to a satisfaction out of view.

I tend to forget the slopes where thinking trails off. I forget sleeping as a means to connect succeeding versions of character. I forget reprieves. The materials of a second wind. I forget the water where it widens to meet the ocean. The level parishes of potato fields reaching to the sky. I forget who it was in a dream that became a cross between Walter Huston and Leo Tolstoy to remind me that rage and affection form the spine of human scale.

There is pleasure in observing memory select and recover, reconnect separate waves curling connecting end to end. When memory reappears having unaccountably lived a deathless and reckless life on its own, it obliterates my forecast of grimy blankness, opening a door to where I live now, speaks through the voice of someone who casually mentions the burrito I ate in the car years ago on the way to see someplace stunning. I can't relive the sting of jalapeno, the avocado spilled in my lap and taste the relief of getting out of the car to look at the canyon fall away into the ocean, the feeling I'll never forget.

We all sit down at the ground level from time to time to see what she sees. She sees a lot more floor than we ever notice. While we are balancing response and responsibility, she is studying the way we cross our feet at the ankles, the worn path in the carpet, the way the wood planks heave and pitch.

She likes to play with specks and gobs testing a world of rudimentary number. All of her blocks, rattles, trains, turtles, beads, bears, picture books and balls have separate measure, distinct volumes. I imagine that for her poetry is oral color, an object's sounds. Tunes envelop her in a thicket of beats. She leans into rhythms and rolls out iambs in babbled sleep. Every newly accomplished word arising from a language she'll forget.

I am writing this while craning over the years that divide a memory of thinking of what it would be like to be measuring this distance between "as it happened" and the mutable table of "now."

I am drinking a beer listening to the clink of glass in sand.

I am following a barely discernible route to a beach of black pebbles, a shore color new to me and as I write it life-lifting again, a perfect reflection.

He completely forgets a child self that once folded a sled into a tree he couldn't avoid while racing downhill in the broadest part of winter. The sled hit the tree with such force he was astounded that he and it did not pass through the trunk, and there was some kind of spontaneous circus inside him pulling stunts, the human cannonball gets inside the lit cannon, soars and survives in a trick of immortality. Vapor streaming from his mouth and flushed body seemed to visibly trace his burning flight outside the commonplace of time that a crashing plate in our neighbor's domestic fight restores to memory, complete. Even his uncle's piercing rebuke: "You may not have broken your neck damn fool, but you sure have broke up that sled."

We are over-rehearsed, accidents don't happen, but are explained, coincidences mount to re-enforce effect. We haven't a clue to where each day begins, here and now or then and there, so we stutter forward, repeating one part, eliding another, remnants of worlds we live only in part.

Correspondence Theory

Dear

The impact of the pipe wrench banging against the copper lines somewhere in the building (the locations change) sets up an irritating vibration that can be heard in all the rooms. The guests have worn out the manager and his assistants with their complaints.

The current group of tourists doesn't come into the lobby anymore since it's only their rooms that are air conditioned and the lobby isn't; the humidity there is thick enough to rub between fingers and produces a harvest of slugs too slow to be anything but friendly, but the brochures don't mention it and looks can deceive.

The bartender, a scrupulous fellow, boils the water he places in bottles of liquor he then reseals and sends to their rooms.

Three days after the first pipe burst, the manager sent men to roll up the carpet and put it in storage. None of the guests have noticed for they seldom venture out there anymore.

Thanks to the facsimiles provided by the Visitor's Center, the traveler can obtain some idea of what the plaza must have been like. The

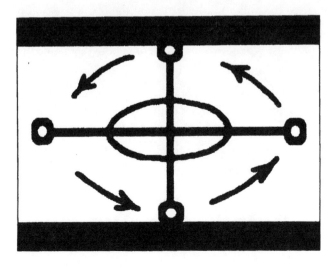

mausoleums suggest heroic themes. White granite columns tapered at the ends bestow a timeless dignity to the facades gleaming white like ice cream beneath the fat noonday sun.

The western edifice shows the scene of the sun fleeing into the horizon pursued by multiplying pigeons. Brass finishings at the end of the hallway give the effect of a tree overcome by its fruit, beneath which are piled classical volumes. The lamps hung directly behind one another are painted nectarine and small birds etched on them create the illusion of a birdbath in a tent.

In the east is the Big Bang himself. Man of stone, the hero stands in the center of a tiled compass, tessellated alpha and omega, cluttered with allusions to the Copernican solar system. Chiselled from one great chunk of granite block, the hero points at (or accuses) the sinking sun in the mural opposite, his finger glitters cruelly. His gaze is alert, if not friendly, polished beams capable of burning through clouds to some spot just beyond the heavens. The base supplies the traveller with open brackets, the hero's years of birth and death, illustrated with supplemental headlines to suggest the feeling of the era compared to here.

At one time the hero had been imprisoned and forbidden pen and paper. He communicated with his colleagues by pouring milk into his rationed bread and taking it with him after meals into his cell. Later he used the milk to write letters on the blank pages of permitted reading materials, smuggling the book to compatriots outside the prison walls. When these pages were held over a flame the words were read by his followers who found their own courage renewed.

Once he was unexpectedly interrupted by a guard while he was writing and acting quickly he ate the bread—from whence comes an expression, similar to one in English, "to eat one's words," but here it has a different meaning.

Dear Dear

I have a feeling I wouldn't like to be in your shoes wherever you are though in order to find you I might have to follow your footsteps, the way one reconstructs the beat of a rumba from an Arthur Murray diagram.

Let me suppose you. You graceful and ordinary remain seated in the plaza waiting for dawn to be rendered around you. A sudden click from the perimeter triggers a chorus of high-pitched birds. Massive dark clouds stretch like continents then break revealing patches of illuminated sky. New smells seep and merge with those of the night—the sun warms the bricks and soil, the heat hangs over hedges and by degree is as vaporous as tea. The wind carries the odor of the lake, of diesel truck and car engines' catarrhal exhaust into the rumble of early morning.

Already the weather is oppressive to you. You watch the queue form at the bus shelters, the women and girls in white blouses and dark skirts, faces youthful and serious. The men and boys also in white shirts, along with khaki pants, carrying shoes, lunch and sometimes an extra shirt in their bags.

You look slightly out of place in this city where people have adopted uniforms, where poverty is disguised by starched white cotton. You shamble along in your loose shorts, walking as if led by your stomach, looking like a natural cousin to the saffron walnut rose umber indigo ebony passer-by, your eyes voracious for kinship.

In search of an ideal resemblance you stop at the first monument you see, shutting the light out.

Dear

Charm is made in the eyes of the observer. Understandably, city officials make use of outside observers, for who could be better qualified than non-residents and tourists who aren't preoccupied with living in the place and therefore are the best observers of its charm?

Movers and shakers draw up maps of detachable parts. Hot, warm and cold zones are identified to guide the visitor, mashing up the formula residents have devised for themselves. Street signs are moved around, and streets renamed so that tourists walk only sanctioned loops. The loops concentrate site of representative locales, ordinarily dispersed through the city, are packed into a pedestrian mail.

But the periphery is everywhere, and its edges are steep. To live with gunshots riding on the night air is to live penned in or penned out of visibility just beyond the horizon, youth stolen or vanished. In this war casualties multiply: one in four in prison, one in four unemployed, one in four with a habit, every square foot to be fought for. In the panic that is no solution, the police pillage and fail to protect; youth stolen by fire; the ranks of the armies swell.

A skilful illusionist can scoop up the details however precarious and put them in for one last spin. So that even as the city teeters on the edge of periodic chaos, even as it appears that present and past lives might become hopelessly idealized or mistaken for each other, even as it seems that the surface is all that is available, it is never impossible to find the perfect official photo:

A skyline illuminated by a bracelet of light. Only a few beyond those awake early in the morning or late at night even realize that the lights of this immense skeleton of a city have to be turned on by someone.

Instead of a city open all night for the purpose of making it run, the
city runs all night so that it can be said to be open.

The cakes couldn't be safer, a sign declares.

The water from the tap is brown and the vents bring noise that
would tumble four or five jars of sleep. The sleep possible in a
postcard in three different languages:

1) a side street of dark august buildings backlit by illuminated glass
tombs,

2) a cross street of market stands upon which there are piles of
colorful bananas and oranges,

3) a main street which serves to welcome and to hide.

The ordinary traveller has to wait until she gets home and has
her film developed to know what she has seen, and concealed,
appearances change that much from stop to stop. No marks on the
body at all.

Dear Dear

Who took off with your map? It's as if your passport were stamped, ready, valid but out of order so you've almost no chance of getting into the place you're at. Your notes lack that competent urgency distinguishable in the letters of a practiced voyeur yet I know your browsing to be merciless.

In an era of palaces inhabited by officials who've inherited their squint you have to do more than scratch the surface.

In the heat of imagining you there, I continually fuel your doings, steal the glances I feel you're not admitting, using the weather as an alibi.

How did it feel when you noticed there were dead and unidentifiable bug parts in the last glass of decent drinking wine (August 1984)? A storm hit a curve and put out the lights on the street (July 1983)? The sky was an immoderate yellow (October 1986)? Was it then you realized the coloration states of mind acquire as they cumulatively knell and that it is heroic to keep your mind open in the hue and din? Saturday (April 18), you went about, jingling the loose change in your pocket, one eye on a book you'd open to get your mind off your poor circulation in hands and feet reading about how Joe Louis could catch houseflies out of the air (one in each hand), so you walked about contrite and modest (3:00p.m.) and idle. You made note of the emotion as you steered a sled downstairs (February 6) which you took as a temporary seasonal aberration and not a disease of the will, the will to then or afterwards be both positive and astonished and positively astonished at how short and complete ordinary life weighs in and is deduced from days fashioned while you're still asleep.

I think it must have been later you decided not to live out this one with your feet up but to take on the subject in stride.

Dear

A parade. The crowns tethered to the disproportionate heads of mascots ride the floats and crash into the tree branches lining the wide avenue where many have assembled and where it is said one obtains the best view. The other heads of state sit in a review stand wearing ceremonial helmets. It is traditional to gather on the corner just across from the stands to catch a glimpse of as many local celebrities as possible. Each year the number of floats increases and the parade has grown into an all-day affair.

Just about every nation is represented. The organizers have varied the order of succession of the parade from year to year. One year, for instance, the floats were arranged by climate: the humid subtropical regions were represented by New Orleans, Beograd, Chungking, and Buenos Aires. The desert by Alice Springs, Yuma, Sofu and Jidda, which sent a float composed of an uncanny white tent emitting white light trimmed with 24-karat gold threads. The climate scheme was attempted in the year the Committee deadlocked on the order of the procession in an effort to avoid the appearance of taking sides in any of the territorial disputes that had erupted. The plan was abandoned once it became clear that not even the weather was an object of neutral participation.

It was soon after that they settled on the lottery system in use today. There have been fewer anomalies using this method; though once an entire 30-minute stretch of the parade rolled by with half a dozen floats from different countries playing generically ethnicized versions of the same song: "The Best of My Dreams for More than A Lifetime Sakura."

While there are still local flourishes that draw crowd approval—the flotilla of bagpipers, the covey of beach dwellers towing sea nets, the gaggle of 12-foot trumpet players and the troop of portable record-player scratchers—many of the entries resort to time-tested images of prosperity.

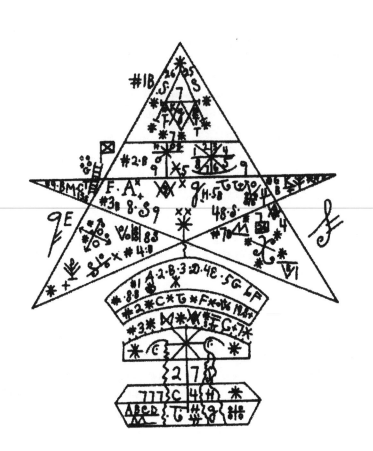

For instance, the local newspaper reported that there was some mild criticism of the Committee for permitting several-score images of sunsets and beaches animated by the charms of Miss (name the country) to advertise a beer company with headquarters in Bavaria.

But that is a minor detraction from a stunning display of invention—a parade that has no match in this century. Not even the Pharaohs had funeral pageants of this grandeur or effort. Nor did they have the range of barbecue, at least a dozen ornament each block. There are four rice and bean stands alone, each with its own proof that arroz is not arroz.

Finally the rain comes. The clouds travel fast and hang over the parade, particularly the nations with the bad luck to be toward the end. This happens almost every year. The clouds break and let down rain over the most steadfast of the litter carriers.

Dear Dear

And if it's heroic gait you want, a labyrinth worthy of your
ingenuity, is there any reason to disembark at most of the stations
that you do, circling the postcard rack prepared to be agreeably
surprised?

Admittedly the station is one of those high-ceilinged relics from an
era before terminals were designed by the literal-minded architects
who design prisons; you like its look of use, from its vaulted ceiling
40 feet above painted with the timorous glances of lewd angels
to its partially clean comfort stations made into two rooms, the
stalls in the rear occupied by boots, luggage and disinfectant. The
pinball machines located between the men's and women's lounges
impartially set at gut level.

From such spangled gloss there's no way to anticipate the self
choreographed stream of pedestrian traffic, the schools of
commuters walking rapidly intersecting paths, who spin out of the
way just before any two streams collide, wearing a look on their
faces as if they'd just woken up.

If you want to let down your guard, your face, in an emergency, now
is the time to drop the mask. You look for a phone booth so you can
leave a message among all the others—autobiographical information
that ventures self-disclosure on found capital. The station is arguably
one of the few places with which a city cannot disguise itself, the
walls and its nightly inhabitants speak volumes. Your suitcase would
do the same for you except you borrowed it.

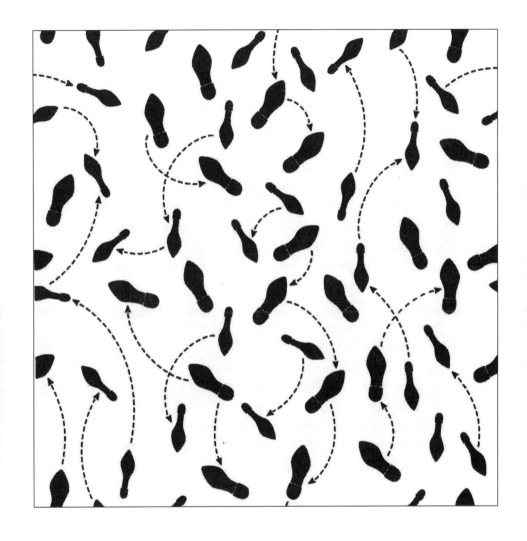

Dear

A hurricane has been forecast for today and as usual the city's population seems to be divided into two camps: those for whom the forecast was a catastrophe they had expected all along and those who have decided to ignore it. The ones who are taking the forecast seriously are—not coincidentally—the city's most vulnerable. For some, catastrophe is an old acquaintance, one storm or another blows the house down, an emblem for all big winds, biblical and legendary. For them, in the days since the forecast was first made, the impending storm has picked up steam in a dozen different degrees of disaster. Large X's have begun to appear on windows, and the food has disappeared from the shelves of supermarkets.

The wind has indeed picked up and trees begin to bend in the park surrounding the lake, the backdrop to the city's main cultural instit . . .

The projector begins to flicker—the movie of the week stalls in its tracks. "Baring the Brain" is the current exhibit in the Museum of Science. Along with the film, the exhibit consists of a long hallway of lit pedestals each of which supports a small glass tank lit from above by spotlights. In each tank the pink and gray matter of famous people rusts, accompanied by a little label.

One brain in particular appears to be a focal point in the exhibit. The pedestal that it rests on is surrounded by little lights embedded in a ring on the floor around its base. Its companion text has been reduced so that the detail will fit on the card.
"The marked development of the pyramidal cells in Lenin's cerebral cortex produced on necessity, an intensification of the general activity of the various divisions of the brain. The large number of paths proceeding from the pyramidal cells and thus uniting portions of the brain otherwise widely separated explains, furthermore, the wide range and multiplicity of his ideas."

In the Hall of Science, the giants sleep waiting for someone to come and misinterpret them. They sleep in violet light, they sleep the sleep of statues, they sleep through sleep and waking; they sleep the sleep of a sleeper who knows how to fall, who has already fallen and no longer worries about falling, they sleep wearing their real faces. The real face is a face made by sleep; eyes closed, but the lights still on and the movie rolling.

One takes this in behind a velvet rope wearing special sunglasses so that the image is 3-D.

Dear Dear

I read looks. While passing a store today I noticed sawdust leaking from a dummy in the display. The figure moved abruptly every few moments as part of its musculature seeped out of its burlap skin.

This is a distillation of your letters, zeroes between the words. All the phrases engaged or apologetic no one could blame you. But finally, this is what I have left of you, a stooping silhouette. I'm asking you to step into the picture, make a guest appearance.

It doesn't improve it but it sure beats reading the impression left in a round-shouldered jacket as you wagging your shoulders in imitation of a serene coastal day on the mesa where we were last August and leaving a pair of shoes on the rocks that complicated the walk back.

I snap the album shut but you're still here in one of the photographs tentatively dipping your foot in the surf wearing as usual your spectator tee shirt.

If we're not who we were then who are we now? Characters multiply as the dubbing editor loses interest. Imagination is not a jinni to slight; often we are forced to consent to the supposition that we are as continuous as others imagine us to be. When you change your mind though you make me an accessory to a peculiar kind of treason.

In lighter moments I recall what I liked about you at a safe distance: the way you carry yourself like a Central African ancestor figure, stomach relaxed, legs bent and parted, and your back curved in a delicate S with no hurry at all.

Secondly you seemed unafraid to call a relic a wreck, a belief a symptom, a skirmish a fool's errand. What some call domestic others call privileged torpor. What some call security from another angle resembles only the knack of imprisoning oneself with as many objects as can be dreamt of.

Similarly l am willing to admit that I often arrange for dramas to be performed with the unwitting assistance of whoever happens to be standing around. That is why I am surprised that you revert to using the descriptions of things to create a war of no practical advantage. In lighter moments, as I was saying, I'm struck by the coincidence. I got tired of waking up in a lake. You were eating out of your hand and not liking it. It's impossible to have a more mutual subject.

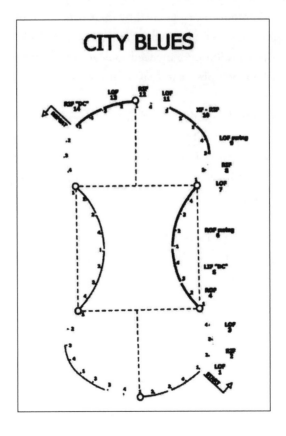

Dear

The forecast was correct but incomplete. The rain soaked the metropolitan region falling in figures—3/4 of an inch here, an inch there—through the night in a period of hours. Damage was limited in even the lowlands. The storm battered downtown however; several feet of sidewalk collapsed under mysterious circumstances and the wreckage from the shore blew inland right into the interchange of the major artery. There were no fatalities and just a few minor injuries.

The newspapers however used the event to anchor a series of stories about the unstoppable: the budget deficit, the local stock market which took a dive (despite unusually high levels of investor confidence), a story about captains of industry, their faces grainy like coal miners, as if the passion of ownership settled in their pores. Each story's importance signalled by their placement on the page, swallowing the smallest story box and a few weeks old, 35 words about a 15-year-old boy sentenced to death for his participation in a murder, which no appeals to reason or justice could prevent.

This at any rate legitimizes the cover story—all the news fit for small print. The news doesn't even begin to touch what's just under the new, and what's there in the papers tends to comes off on the fingers. People believe they may find a free press if they could just find the right reading room.

The free press would have to be written untranslated in different languages, a few of which have never before been transcribed. In the free press everything would have to be aggressively connected or related or mismatched, to make organization transparent where substance is not. In the free press people try themselves out for the first time, by testing their point of view.

The photos on the pages of the free press suggest the human without letting them be mistaken for more than what they are—a moment of the person. In this press, the articles are a prelude to induce the reader to meet the reader face to face. The first reader introduces herself as a citizen. The second reader sees that he and the first reader have something in common, something to talk about. Other readers join in. Together they interview the editorial staff to see why it is that journalists want to write about their street. The columns are fact checked by primary school students and lead to new asides.

The index of current events is eclectic where subjects mostly hold their place by figures of speech; self-admitted fragments in incidental parentheses one after the other to stand for an approximately complete choice.

Dear Dear

I too have a confession to make. While I accuse you of not being yourself, I myself am contrary. When my habits are pointed out to me I deny the fit. Facsimiles make me itch. In my book there's no room for a superficially reasonable description, the person taken out of turn relies on placing them in the hereafter unamendable, stabilized, modest, extreme, negative, naked, posing, unrecognizable, looking out of both sides of her head.

The police put out an all-points bulletin for the angel of anger, the double of themselves: they look as if they might be violent. The definition of this violence is always the same: his eyes are red, his teeth go way back in his head, a crocodile about to swallow his own tail.

I turn sideways. I dodge and feint. Tell me I am sensitive or tyrannical and I soon shall find a new way to fill in the blank. If I am told that I am orderly I'll confound the simplest grocery list, and if I am told I like my bit of comfort, I'll make the best of a week without bath or comb. I flatten and fold over. I spindle. I follow orders.

Come tell me that I am homely and I shall brighten.

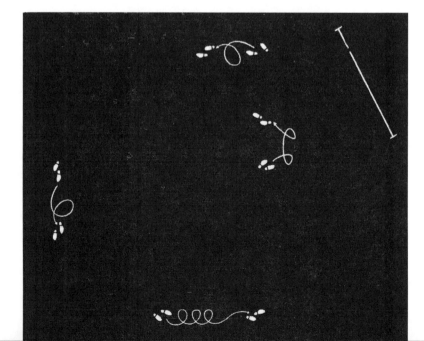

Dear Dear

A tour of the plant bristles with indirect riches. Here, yolks are placed back in their eggs by machine. The process of extraction, condensation and reconstitution is a product of the most advanced technology: a recipe of molten steel and cast-metal fingers performing the delicate task of holding shells and albumen steady while cylinders pour cholesterol-free yolks into their centers. Less egg is needed to make eggs.

The work force is divided according to the length of their sleeves. The long sleeves are managerial. The short sleeves are the line workers and the women wear special collars.

Each room of the plant shares the same acoustic mission: to rearrange space. Thus you can be standing right next to someone and you might as well as be listening to a cat, while across the room someone can hear you think.

Every day hundreds of millions of square feet of eggs are delivered to this plant which has the exclusive right of production. The people at the desks supervise this process. Behind every desk is a long waiting list, and everybody knows it. This tends to make the young cautious and the empowered anxious about who's waiting to fill their shoes. The supervisors tend to drive away potential visitors by burying their heads in charts that track egg production.

As in many places where people's motion is intended to be more or less constant, excessive loitering is discouraged by ambient light music. These are versions of masterpieces—the landscape of the William Tell Overture rendered by a chorus of whistlers.

Once the tape has turned off at the end of a shift, the absence of sound lifts scratches from the lens, the surroundings seem dangerously legible. Stainless-steel surfaces reflect so much light they ring as they gleam. The smell in the plant changes too, an olfactory siren sharp enough to make you lose your balance. And the most distinct sound is the noise of the heart pumping buckets to make the stare fearless in the face of returning sensation.

Dear Dear

You mean feelings. Did you know that in English there are more words referring to external objects than there are words to refer to internal states?

Faces convey immediate meaning while words take their time to reach you. Eighty or so muscles in our skin slack or tense in a kinetic vocabulary that could go on without a comma. In the fiction of your letters how do you punctuate your body english, how do you wear the stamp of things seen?

A man I know has a stare that means business. He has two kinds of stares, actually, business and pleasure. Most people trapped in his gaze try to fight back; they either break its hold by laying flat and still against whatever background is handy, so that voila they are part of the picture or they try to divert his attention. But few try to return his view blow for blow.

Words are just paper clips in this kind of encounter, holding the place in a book to let you know where you're at. The stare demands a story and the story demands boundaries. You stay inside a landscape of it, you a body hold up your end of the conversation. You a tree locked inside the body of a tree. Finally you stick out your neck.

The perfect proof of desire is risk. A star is only an example. Stare long enough and the star blinks. Desire teaches thought to think out loud. Original looks bolt from the eyes.

Surplus Landmarks
(Union Square Blues)

The square was a rectangle, a plaza-sized flower box painted
concrete to catch the tilt of a risen noon. When the old Klein's died
it spread its architecture of elasticized articles west. It came down
to make way for a three-masted brick ship of progress, each mast a
realized boast, filled to the sky with paying customers. Even the sun's
been rewrapped, by reinforced steel and plate glass; its beams splay
the fence.

Little Bombay sucks her coffee regular squinting in awe at the
newly configured sky. How do they keep it up? There's a limit to
space-time logic but you can bend the rules to make a profit. They
sell four quarters for a dollar, it's a fact, and the wheels within
wheels slow the traffic. The goods are guarded by club throwers,
as shoppers assume the position, inch by angry inch, past gloves
without fingers, and hats with antennae piled in heaps on the streets
for sale. The crowds shod in running shoes scramble to match an
introspection, snatch an object from the jaws of its price. It's an
express stop though the clock was shot down from the sky. It's a real
contradiction, no two ways about it.

Surplus Future Imperfect

When the smoke lifted there was no promised land in sight. No place to make a phone call. No lounge to use the soap in. No holy days, no spirituals, no speeches intended to solder you to earth. No seams between the excuses and platitudes. No reason to get up. No stops. No long nights of man-made objects. No more of the same. No difference. No table of contents just a list of demands. No anecdotes, we were getting paid by the hour. No benefits, we were temporary workers. No music, corporate ambience. No seat belts, the entire world seemed unsafe. No geography, tourists were made at home with identical decor. No libraries, information out of the picture. No thought police, we all became deputies, we never let a line blur.

Surplus

Equals the difference between beginning to wake up and beginning
the day. Surplus equals the pause before the day's contents are
anticipated in detail that overspills its container. Surplus equals
the day through an open door, the relics of dream littering the bed,
antecedents before they are doctored by conclusions.

She listens to herself telegraph. What cracks, emotions overlap?

Verse

It's all in profile
what the shadows cast
on the floor. Can you see?
When pushed to the wall
paper our habits seem trivial,
a record of the body's lost accidents.

We found that we could not be strangers
anymore, nor could we pose
randomly in our affection ducking
behind a turn of mood.
Instead we carried ourselves

unrehearsed into the arms of the unexpected
Continuity, using our sense to head
where we are going.
Every story has its campaign to win.
Missing numbers, interfering digits.
We work from the beginning to the back
end tracing where the author left her
prints on the text, her surplus

divinity. And when the right word
appears out of nowhere
it leads back here.
What word were we looking for?
Fire. In this light we appear

To be doing what we want, waving
the baton with the mind. If you want
to move your feet find something

there over the bridge of your
nose to attract you. Choose your
own words to hear yourself speak.

Light is composed by experience. Without correction it stands still
and is almost invisible collecting dust. Without it, we tend to see
lumps, and not the landscape the voices of people fall out of. The
light in the brain is you.

The net

Momentary wind in my ears during
the channel crossing.
We hang onto each other
massage the exchange of heat:
(radiant, unlit aromatic
Exclamation.

Look.

Look back to back on it
where our embrace has brought us,
to the other side of beloved,
behind the face
within inches of an extreme
edge of our most forward selves.

Suits us, don't you think—
to be that close to living
skin not indentured to the imagination.

You stir again, or is that me,
unwinding the elastic bits;
both of us tied in such unexpected
places
the curve of a back a waiting bracket

Our silhouettes enfold, back from exile,
we find form: our legs, thighs
a free substance returning to liquid;
an even moisture you lay down
paints my skin,

rinses the label and slips me a peel,
rises from my hands, my feet, and
gives you back your sense of touch.

A storm
close enough to tip us over:
love without a net.

Woman, with Wings

The way out of the library isn't always
clear. Victory, or so she calls herself
drives with me. We move closing the
zipper across the landscape, joining
two sides of an emotion together.

Up ahead, at the fork, causality
breaks into a side effect. We interrupt the
librarian's silent monologue. It drains
his face of animation, sucks the air
from the room.

His figure bars the exit like
a bad habit. It is possible to train these
associations whether you like them or not.
With practice you can predict defeat, or
summon the sun
rise over the scene murderously.

Work is pushing past resistance,
past the sense
it has all been written
before, spilling off the inventory shelves.

Sometimes you can read
with the headlights on, sometimes
you can drive to moods for which
no correlates exist, only curves, shaded
paths in the wilderness, occasional plots of
land ignored by absentee owners.

The cars ahead of us have disappeared.
Finally the way is clear, we have come to a way out:
past the flocked walls, the manipulated
seams, past the unzipped feeling, the tacit
violence between its teeth,
the trick with the mirrors and speed.

Afterword

Curves are sharp and the
noises mysterious. I close my
eyes and I'm still coming around
the curve. Afterimage on retina
park. And I don't know what will
happen next. There is no guide to
context for this leap to land into.

Rigor of rope and railing, failing
that's what parallel
lines we keep.

Piece Logic

House of Broken Things

In a country where it is common to assume that a new
place gives you a new origin, leading to a different set of
titles and possibly more exalted circumstances. In a country that
lives on headlines, where explanations are clocked to incorrect
metrics set to bracket disproportionate measures of hectic and unchecked
brutality; In a country where a foreigner is welcome as s/he is
generic or naturally naturalized and numbered

.

It is customary to give every object its count; to number
the citizen and her possessions in order by constitution to
limit liability by label and name, every object passing through
enumeration is certified and citizens are surrounded by
certified belongings, a horde of things indemnifying identity.*

*Part mammal. Part tiller of soil. Part toiler of affect, conveyor of a
frictionless life. Part legend etched in landmark. That part is glossed. Part
object of loathing, of envy or lust. Part removed body from haunt and taint,
mute stones on stained land. Part invented Tuesday to reconcile Wednesday's
body count where monuments dismember memory.

The objects are tested and assigned an incarnation, and objects so tested are given a seal, an assignment of limited durability, by the House of Broken Things, a holy affiliated division of its original

The objects arrive shrink wrapped, adamant, brilliant,
resembling an illuminated text, ready to be admired.
The tags claim the high ground of indestructibility,
shamelessly wrapping themselves in the symbols of
great empires, pyramid, halo, iron cross, to disguise
their true membership in the atomic kingdom, with
its currency of rust, dust and ashes.

The lead researcher collects the eternity tags tied onto the toes of things waiting to be tested. She collects them because it reminds her of the truth of things, that objects self-destruct from the day they roll off the assembly line, moving guilelessly toward object death.*

*No sentimentality is permitted in the House, and it is only
sentimentality that confers value that survives calculation, put to the
side and subtracted from the total weight.*

Welcome to the House of Broken Things, a holy inde-
pendent affiliate of the original, where we test more than
3 million products each year. We are more than our tests,
We think of ourselves as investigators into the limits
and possibilities of material reality. Though we shatter
our share of televisions, and toasters, we like to think
of ourselves as the repositories of incontestable evidence.
A source of consumer and existential confidence.

time management

Piece work measured in throat sung pop anthems,
topple silence, unstring the
dots, simulate temptation
disconnect, to invent this life in phantom objectivity
step outside, as if the leash could stretch that long, and
look back in at the heap, uncoil a pile of props
instruments for gauging speed for this atomic clock's
devotion, a box of crayons to color
trees that break up the sky
lines in the hand that become branches
fissures in the rocks to trace the confessions of water
Overtime, the figure x forever practical, turned on its head.

Object Authority

We conduct three basic tests-what, how and who tests or
What tests: what is safe?
How tests: how does it open?
Who tests: who does it serve?

So strong is the force of habit, a force summoning the
rapacious maw of open quotes in the house of broken things,
there are objects that don't need to be fixed.

She responds to the call to fix, even if it hasn't been made
to exact the creatures of melancholy and deduct them.

From a multiplying inventory, the world's useful inventions
forego cosmology to embrace the royalty of the material
world to eliminate the need for a divine form.

A national standard of measurement is created to shelve
the volumes, miles of appearances and possibilities.

Bread dough machines, rice cookers, vegetable sculpting
tools, devices used once a year or sent to siberian flea
markets in spring to call like a siren to the hapless.

The object authority conducts an object theater, a rehearsal
of the evidence.

The house of broken things promises to ban objects
offensive to good sense. Promises by the row what no
money can buy, belonging.

A club whose membership sings a mythical octave of har-

monious families and no awkward silences. The dipthong
disappears into a hard d, replacement of the tube amplifier
by the chip.

The house of broken things preserves broken links, ties to
origins and derivations.

There is a committee of unauthorized things.

Millions of parts connecting characters and miles of appliances,
lining the intestinal maze of its imposing architecture.

In the bunkers on a green hill in Virginia.

The floors support enormous weight, heavy machinery on
gray and rubberized floors.

Creating a catalog is labor-intensive, recording the range and
characteristic of every object with precision, noting the subtle
changes in consumer tastes:

The evolution of harvest gold to tuscan amber, the journey
of avocado to celery. The permutation of buttons and speeds,
convenience and silence, the volumes of clean segregated from
chaotic dirt, the aroma suggested by model names.

The customs of each century preserved, its marketing of absolute
obedience to the thing as it mutates, as it was meant to be.

History not only written by the victors, but revised and trade-
marked by them and their revisions happily bought up by the
conquered as regurgitated shrink wrapped kente cloth toaster
ovens, adhesive backed ikat on temperature control waffle irons.

Collusion picked up off a shelf, the good life with a stamp.
Heaven's own brand.

The house of broken things certifies status, a reference
collection to be cited in courtrooms, schools, torture halls,
parliamentary situations. Lighting up the corners of the English
speaking world.

Administering
the Atomic Kingdom

Recently the government cut
funding for the laboratory.
Elected officials have sent
staff to poke around and they
have written reports asking
unanswerable questions, such
as why do we need a house of
broken things. Surely we have
enough broken things already.
Things always break, why fund
what any infant knows as a fact?

The facts are the facts and these
facts are buried in appendices
that outnumber the pages of
their books.

At the house of broken things,
reports cost hundreds of dollars
per page and the pages stack up.
The practitioners have a dazed
look about them prowling their
labyrinthine laboratories. The
corridors are a colorless twilight
linking labs bursting with life
science, cook with chemistry,
count beans

through unimaginable numbers.
The tools of destruction require
careful oiling and preservation.

Ever more precise numbers of
iota management fill sheds,
cubicled staff respond to
endlessly possible inquiry
stretching mile after expensive
mile. The house is no bargain, it
pays full price for its objectivity.

This in a country of popular
imagination, where the facts are
determined by election and the
elections have fixed results based
on the blessings of the highest
bidder.

This is a country within a
country, where the citizens are
numbered in innumerable ways.

Beltway commuters enveloped
in brown paper trench-coats,
curiosity at a remove (a pesky
gland), pass the windows of
their fellow farmers. The views
are piled high with files, spare
sweaters, seasons of office
detritus, boxes, warranties,
sales slips, running shoes, lunch
menus. All bury the riddle of
ink, typewriter keys that change
the subject, when the author is
not looking.

This is the world of objects
we have made, and their silent
rebellions are conducted under
our very eyes. The inventory
gets out of line, undermines
truth by numbers. There are
unauthorized breaks on the
line between one thing and
another. The temperature
turns out to have a profound
impact on the nature of things:
winter storms tie up traffic. The
original instructions are lost
rendering even the most precise
coordinates almost useless for
these things far from self-evident
are undecipherable without
them; all they are good for is
company, and they do not speak.

The knee bone is connected to
the thigh bone and the thigh
bone to the hip bone, eventually
connects to constantly moving
persons. In search of truth by
numbers, while everywhere the
house leaks cold air.

Wage to labor measured: Paid
hours zero down, made of
maximized moments, only 15
seconds allotted per screw,
there's little left to take home.
The clocks arc locked to tick
only the time objects keep,
whisked to the world shelves.
they can't keep stocked, the
goods sell so fast, manufactured
by invisible hands.

Invisible Hands

Trade down the block or round the world, down the food chain
from forward to back to escape the air grabbing heat, the crop
failing, the monsoon in June, a fluke of the weather, a storm of
flowers, whipped into a rain that claims the last village.

Residents head out to the city to make money. They never make
the money they seek instead they make key chains, sneakers,
baseball gloves, flame proof nightwear, transmissions, stereos,
computer chips, Gap jeans, rugby polo shirts, dolls with the
features of norteamericanos or slave girls or Indian princesses
living their lives in legend unlike their own except for an un-
locatable middle.

Just in time, the chain continues unbroken, to unwind the thing after
the thing, a line of never broken nouns. If it breaks we fix it quick
so the chain can never be broken, even if it shouts out, a chorus set
to shovel. The rocks never seem to disappear but become dust, a
dust that lasts from morning to mourning, chained to a logic we are
doomed to follow.

Invisible hands rice the peas, spice the rice, circle the turns, turn
on the presses, raise the letters, letter the spaces, address the edges
before they bang into one another, mask the connections.

Invisible hands milk the spill, ship the ink, jump the rope, rip the
chute, lay the trail, time the tear, eye the glass, bat the wing, bat the
lash, brown the tan, fiddle the styx, ride the herd, read the horde,
hear the roar, read the dim, damp the rhyme, rhyme the orange,
toast the storage.

Carry the thread, thread the vowels, stall the calls, pour the molds, powder the walls, dent the bins, stamp the bills. Core the questions, comma the nouns, time the charts, corner the squares, square the curves, loosen the jaws, spill the beans, bell the cats, feed the beasts.

It's years before a family will follow off the edge of the ramp into this putative new life, where the past has vanished and the present is all time charts. Marked invisibly.

Only visibly hot, in a red dark of selective vision, in plain sight and out of sight, one hand trying to clap the other.

As in the phrase, "give me some skin" the slap of palms right hand to right hand empty, no weapon here, we come in peace we come out of the hypnotic circle that orbits and holds us in constant bind of stick 'em up and lap dancing, out of rigged destiny, across the violent border of property and oblivion, until hands can be detected in the bric a brac of the world.

Proof

Proof that we live in a broken world and a broken world is unlivable.

Proof that the carrot turns into the stick and vice versa. Proof that that seems normal, self-sufficient.

Proof that we sometimes destroy things that are broken and can't be fixed and sometimes fix things because to live with them broken is unthinkable.

Proof that we switch roles, sometimes to destroy things that are broken and can't be fixed and sometimes to live with things that are broken because to fix them would be unthinkable.

Proof that we learn to live with the unthinkable.

Rectangles in tangerine, orange and persimmon fall into place, take our names, simulate full hands. Proof that having full hands leaves no time for questions.

Proof that we can't help grabbing the sharp end, even when all the warnings are there.

Proof that we find the hot water, the hot water finds us.
Proof in the tongue of ruin and burn. Fluent in the language of minus.

The trees have fallen and the forest comes apart.

Proof then by reading it on paper. Proof in unmarked bills. Line by line our eyes fill up with witness: Mornings as clear as glass.

Can stones be far behind?

Household Gods

The shoemaker's children have no shoes. Outside the house of broken things, she never knows how to choose appliances, when she sees them now fully dressed, off the examining table. She barely recognizes them in their bright packaging, surrounded by snowy white Styrofoam and suggestively cut cardboard. Even the relatively denuded model appliances on the store shelves seem worlds away from the electronic anatomies she and her colleagues disassemble and reconstruct. They seem coy, the way the naked body when clothed or partially clothed is coy. The bodice frames the breasts, the thong nuzzles the thigh where it meets the coil, the strap caresses the shoulder as it falls. She is momentarily baffled and aroused by the come-ons of appliances in the market place, shudders in shameless steel.

Not only the modern appliances, but even the old ones she sees at the flea markets on the weekend, the way their belts are strapped, discreet bits visible from below, the springs locked in visor grips, stiff joints tense, compact weight registering in the palms in the tips of her fingers as she tries all the buttons.

When she finally makes it to the appliance section of the K-Mart to replace that microwave or toaster she is as covert in her investigations as a business man in a suburban tit bar.

Reinflatable happiness. The toaster breaks and she cruises the aisles of the megastores looking for a new one. Sometimes she looks, even if she doesn't need a new toaster. On such days, she feels especially dirty, doesn't want to be recognized.

The salesman breaks the strap on the package to extract a toaster to display to her. "The cord's pretty long" he mutters as he unwraps the tie holding the electrical cord. "It'll fit any outlet, see like this" and he demonstrates. "Toaster ovens generally fall into two ranges, cheap and expensive. You know, like a convection type, that'll roast a meat or stew, and defrost food, that's going set you back some ducats:'

Rapid even heat. Dry heat safely contained. A dizzying heat, heat of no radiance, heat cubed, multiplied without becoming spent. The salesman describes the oven in a manner that defies physical law. It supplies perpetual heat, natural law broken in this disordered universe. For some reason, this sounds just right to her.

At home the thing breaks and she can never find the warranty. Just like the rest of us. Concentration destroyed by sirens. The effects of the lack of effect. It doesn't plug in as advertised. It burns the toast. It bites the hand that feeds it. It remains bone cold.

The washing machine churns and walks across the utility room in agitation. It throws up soap suds and unaccountably has accidents on the floor. The iron scorches and whistles, never means what it says, rumples the linen and burns the nylon.

The microwave sings and hisses and melts the plastic containers it tends. The refrigerator never ceases humming, sometime breaking into post-modern cold jet choruses. All the food placed in it spoils. The dishwasher breaks glasses in fits and puts food on the plates that have been thoroughly rinsed before they were placed in the racks. She's never had a CD player that liked the music she likes to play.

High Anxiety

We are careful to never take a trip together, especially the parents, both at once, by airplane or train. We leave separately on separate dates, and meet at a location we don't disclose until within an hour of our rendezvous.

We stay away from windows, also large public places and famous spots, Grand Central might as well be another galaxy, and also Yosemite, the Parthenon, Victoria Falls; and Shea Stadium. The Amazon is a remote possibility.

We only eat food from cans or sealed in packages. Food that has been registered and has a traceable record. Unfortunately, we had to eliminate any food that is red.

As a precaution we have set up our own cell with bars, a uniform and an alarm system. We hope all of this is enough to protect the life we have built together—its routines: wood, rock, paper, scissors, the threads.

Tin Gods

It's the opposite of a mirror: the pictures talk back &
don't say what you think
the flowers fall they have no choice
birds take on spring duty, house wrens the color of toast.

Stone cornices seen for the frozen waves that they are
spirals locked in time rippling outward—architecture's
ligature of fire escape shaped like bat cages

In this the land of holy boasts, helicopters hover hundreds of feet
above tree level like bumble bees stationary and furiously
buzzing. Land of pocket parks and petit plazas lead to

ringside landmarks, into or out your neighbor's window
you don't find them they find "you"
watching,

rehearsing a victory speech; the old emancipation
granted but judiciously contained—
approximated but molded like a foam obelisk

or faux pyramid a plaster of mismatched parts, the tin gods
appear to say what you think but net out

the spill in rain, bruise of sunshine, the unlocateable peeping sound
from the misplaced watch, not to mention the joy jolted from
the seams between you and them—our children murmuring in their sleep.

Arcade

first words

Night exits fast
to sky painted
huge ahead of itself
the morning appears
an alien character
mauve on the set
where I am the Sunday
company
glad to be a passenger
slumped
on a wobbling planet
tilted in risen dawn.

I stray from my lines
my mind
a moving target
Stand
speaking to the sky
even if its lights are punched out
Night falling into dawn
the shadows change
what's under stones or understates
the tension of what's concealed
and what's shown.
the words that return in the face
the face of the familiar
defend the overwritten

the words at the center
or at a dead end
use grammar to parse their decease

the words that unbutton the
pants of ardent description

the words leading from one thing to the next
shift as you enter

the words in bones
stand for what they are part of

the words that overstate
hyperbolize

the words that give nothing
beyond the marks carried in ourselves
ensure we don't spill a drop

Coronary Artist (2)

Though what I live now is ordinary, I have lived through the glory of numbers. I have visited zero in the sense of absolute beginning to watch fate bleed uncontrollably through a vast chain of explanatory footnotes wound like a bandage over the simplest matter.

I have resisted the power of spelling and broken the spell of pronouns inventing continuity where persons and personalities change sides. I have peered through a keyhole into that narrow room, history, where it is happening to someone else upstairs overhead wearing heavy shoes.

Pathetic, awkward, overdoing it, thumping around breaking into static, fend off the eros to which we react, never initiate, grabbing instead what stales our everyday, our faded monotony. Who wouldn't kick in their sleep and wander off the path of managed impulse? Who wouldn't aspire to become an alien in their own language for a moment to lose the feeling of being both separated and crowded by their experience?

The flowers wear pink as if coming down with the fever. The first to let go were the attributes losing hold of their objects. I was there on my tippy toes feeling thickness leave me, my palms turning into asterisks, my bent arms into commas.

A little display of excitement waved, produced in me the memory of companionship. I watched myself follow the wave and disappear over the crest of a hill in a stuttering laugh.

My back bristled with the urge to give chase, to demand a say, to reconfigure paradise with perfect weather and regular elections. But the distances confused me. Where I stand now, I shout out of my body armor. I whisper parts of the roar.

Coronary Artist (3)

In a dream I go to a room of spare parts.
We apply porcelain to our hair.
There are special scholars who study temples.
Someone sweeps shoulder-length tresses across the floor.
Arms in varieties of salute beckon, bent and dimpled.
I have one leg up.
I'm not fast enough and they take the other.

They hand me costume lips.
My ears are festooned.
What remains after my waist is whittled is little more than a
functioning crease.
I bat my eyes to practice fascination.
but of particular concern is my hair, my hair, my hair.
so dry it crackles, as it is French-twisted and lacquered bright
vermillion.
With this hair I stop traffic, eliminate the inconvenience of
passageways,
duration between significant events, for something is always
happening,
as I travel through mirrors, I'm on the subway platform and the
train comes, it's the A, the IND. I get on.

Magritte's Black Flag

There will be delays this morning on the Number 4 express train to Woodlawn. Express passengers are advised to wait for the Number 5 or 6 running on the local track.

The Number 6 local will also be delayed this morning due to unusually high volume on the local track. Delays are expected through the morning.

Passengers are advised to take alternate routes to their destination, such as the N or R lines. The N & R lines have been switched to the LL tracks to make room for additional 5 & 6 trains making all BMT stops.

The LL trains have been moved to the Number 1 line. The Number 1 is on the 2 and the 2 is on the Three.

The Number 7 has been suspended this morning. To get to Queens, please go upstairs and get a transfer for the shuttle bus to the F train which is providing temporary service to Queens Plaza.

Passengers traveling to Long Island City must complete their travel by 7 P.M. tonight when all service to Long Island City will be discontinued. Passengers wishing to continue to Long Island City are advised that there are buses at the 59th Street Bridge. Bus schedules have not yet been made public.

Starting with A

She passes through pockets of warm air in a cold season, assailed by night noises, sounds in a correspondence based more on bravura than the contents of this failing world.

Start with A as in ANT, and give to every terror a soothing name.

Death is a white boy backing out a lawnmower from the garage, staring down the black girl's hello, silently re-entering the cool shell of his house.

Is it an accident? She is working without quotes, never looking down.

The sunlight thickens at the end of the day bringing the edges of things nearer, sharp laughs that break the honeyed silences.

In night country all routes are approximately marked. There the exact temperature of the prison can be felt, the degrees distancing "home" from its public relations and denial. At night the shortest moments rustle in their chains; the invisible blends in.

Arcade

Blistering routine, I muse through events until I'm in deep, so deep, I no longer notice the D or the P, the down down dirty dirt, the relative positions, who's behind the barbwire and who's in front, within and without, gagged angels of liberalism burying the hatchet in the social body, leaving it for dead.

I don't notice the clock, cartwheeling its way to the end of the millenium, the fix in the race, nor the tick in platonic bombs beneath the feet or an undecided public standing on a ledge.

Anymore.

I swim in this lack, swimmer in a salty non-solution, current events on one side, the present on the other, running neck and neck. Non-events sell newspapers but are curiously unreported, not even as consolation for the tense freedoms we don't miss.

Each day salved by a dozen analgesics applied to my sore spots, from my hemorrhoids to my teeth set on edge, I travel to the "World of Work!" to face down the day to day until one of us surrenders. I go for bonus points by being closest to the train door when it enters the station. But the mood wears off and I can smell the stench of the anesthetic sting my nose as I begin the count backwards into a childhood powerlessness, a childhood where authority defers to your wishes to the point of forgetting about them.

I want to pull a tantrum, the emergency cord, slam on the brakes of this moving forward which is really a standing still at the station. The conductor comes on the intercom and intones an explanation as if he were the narrator and I were the ghost in unrelated and overlapping plots.

We wait in the dark. We cannot tell if we are at the brink again or just in the middle. Are we on an incline or are we stranded, far away from any suitable destination?

We try to scan the headlines at a polite distance. Of course no one believes a word of what we know will be written there, even when they thrown the predictable live bait before the blood-bored crowds. We wear our indifference with dignity, in fact, it gives us dignity, separates us from those who've been taken in or begun to fade in the glare of the bright arcade lights, the rings and buzzes—crowding those who live the war game instead of play it, just past the point where a thought can be followed.

Coda

Against the complete dark, against bureaucratic seizures of the possible, against the body buckling itself against the irregularities of desire, the multiplication of parallel lines meet over the fold in the mind, just past the point where a thought can be followed, where the curve is constant, motion displacing motion, checkers in black spaces and fluctuating light. . . .

the voice of no

No need to be contrary, I put on a face.
No use for muscle, the workers stand on line for hours.
No need to read, 24 hours of the shopping channel.
No fire, we have the illusion of doing what we want.

Is it any way to talk with your tongue pressed against glass?
The tv set is barking this Sunday morning off
when we acquire an instant memory,
and round language, where the ends justify the ends.
We rummage among the many
unplugged connections

looking for that darn
fraction of a percent of the landscape
you say it is possible to live in,
who will miss
it when we divide up
the sun, devour the
young rather than
give up our good seats.
The postcards
are brought out,
the lp is skipping
and anyway
rescue is sure to be slow.
In place of a raft
we paddle
ladders past the litter of drifting bodies.

Science of the Concrete

At first you see
only its description
the skin
a container of its
umber
its beauty
folded into the carved
surface
then you don't know
what you are seeing
whether it is the object
you see or the shadow
you see
falling
completely before
the body stops
falling
in its dream
that hangs
there.

and when it is done
the statue appears
as a couple
still sitting
there never
breaking
an embrace in
one piece.

II
its "back" away from you
so you "know" which way
to face, and with what
attitude
in the language of backs
to regard as complete
whether ambidextrous or not
whether we exaggerate
the numbers of sides
or smooth the planes
of slow shifting hips.

the unseen part
is a controlling force
over bodies written off
as repetition of the already seen
degrees of sex
and color
to be held against
backed
against
the wall
and halved
unrecognizably
halved.

people "make"
the people around them
and they write
to write
the reader
out of retreat,
out of distant austerity

concealing this same
fragile activity
people make
each other
part by part
then whole
into *whole*

Fortune

We haven't entered enough contests and won. But we'll correct that—we'll break the bank and go from one to the other, sweepstakes winners, lotto lovers, zero demons, a terrible crew of arrivistes, swilling seltzer and ordering books they don't have in the kitchen. Watch out. We will leave a winning streak in our wake, like the sign of Zorro, like a hunter with her ear to the ground, looking for the next roll of dice, like a window you can see *through*.

Go ahead, make some noise. This morning lives for racket, it makes the sun rise faster, part fact, part fiction. We wake up to make ends meet—to make ends meet.

Personal

Logic seeks object to undergo rigorous eye witness:
the rest a test of patience.
Objects collected: cloak of visibility,
hypothetical continuity,
simultaneously independent propositions;
grammar—a cause.
No reasonable emotion refused.

Madame Narcissist

I have the power of simultaneous affect; it breaks off in a smile.
I adore the arbitrary embrace of *you*.
I light up the reader.
Even my dark side is worthy of study.
Every day my pennies turn a thought.
I see my ideas everywhere, on the brink of worldwide acceptance
and potential profit.

I believe my silence speaks volumes.
I have as many layers as any serial killer.
I'm in the moment.
I play that game when I'm bored.
I believe the story about the father who drove to work and left his child
in back in the car seat all day.

I believe in personal contact.
Nothing escapes my notice.
Everything around me is subject to decay.
I've lost count.

I teach these kids more than they need to know.
I have the same number of stitches.
I don't know how it happened, I was just standing here.
I know they are after me.
I know the author.
I already have a better angle on this.
I do not go out of my way so I am never out of the picture.

II
I am sentenced to think in lines running away and toward radical
detachment, where "I"s lock.

A tractor song imitating life (art) running down the rows, I think,
of selective flamboyance.

Phone calls preempt the buzzless space around me.
The trail gives out; vines cover it.

I sweep up the impulses of intangible dread, along with the prior
generations' conviction that the rules of destiny entail implacable
random betrayal, where no good deed goes unpunished. Others are
mourning dead ironies. How are these truths truly related?

I seek legibility.
I read clouds; continental doubt.
I tend to color the facts, unbinding private property so it multiplies.
I hold on to time; I summon the past. Still my gaze simulates
connection.
In sleep the brain wills it, my fingers picking out the thread.

so sex, the throne whose abrasions we crave

today or tomorrow I will shove the books off my bed
and pick up my lap and go somewhere where I have longed to go.

I will make myself narrow and let another body pass through.
I will let go of the wheel for a moment.

Sing road hymns over the bumps.
Chat over the table feeling the heat rise.

I will let the odd curve merge.
I will be the first to touch.

I will be the touch, before it is dry.

**after Baudelaire's
"The Muse for Hire"**

Oh confused and demon heart
that mounts and pilfers hours;
the calendars are clogged too.
The years have 13 months each,
while January to January parades
lashed to the inevitable
in winter's anonymous darkness.

The hours are noiseless, the sores insensible,
the tissues of connection reel
as if in rented tuxedos,
droopy-eyed, a drunken brush away from violence.

Rein them in tight.
Don't trouble what doesn't break.
Don't violate the sense of purse or secondhand pleasure
recalled or lamented
that ring of truth and other
undetonated hazards.

How beautiful the reasonable grip of stock behavior
like an infant who leans and chants grasping
the cross of her crib
and springs tedium from the trap
but cannot escape herself.

Or sitting back, joins
eating to appetite
her laugh to pleasures

administered in low voltages
or her faith to the efficient
reduction of riddle.

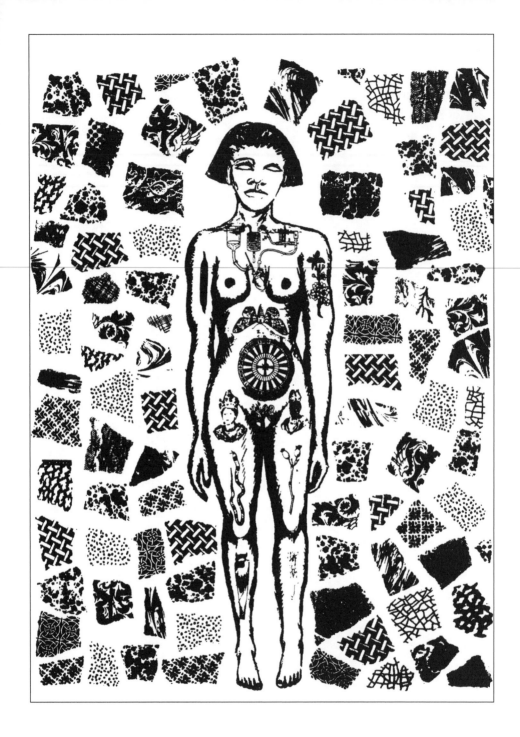

Biographical Suite

1. Ecstasy

What have we to look forward to but old age
an unfolding of the flesh into some foreign package
whose stamps we barely recognize
whose worries are like lint we pick up from nowhere
the scar of it from no accident we can recall
but obtained in the dark, in the dark
theater we embrace a faded script.

I can't explain it. I looked up from the page and
found myself fully grown.
It lasted for about an hour.

Here's my strength—to follow the meaning
even as it stands zig zag along the sheer edges
of sight; the brittle garlands of thought
jagged-toothed scale the horizon.

Noted for my level head
even among these unfinished songs.
Instead of planning beauty, I, as they say
"let it happen." Let eyes connect the dots.
Air connive with the invisible.
Ecstasy is blind and moves on wings, torn feathers.

2. Shadow Box

Situation reversed, my father dies when he is young. Not me. He dies
a boy, though he died my parent, a middle-aged man. The boy dies
only a few days ago, I am told. The boy dies in me.

He is a young man of uncertain prospects and ambition. What dies? The boy dies because he is careless. Because of something he forgets to do. Was that his first death?

My father dies a young man, just a few days ago, tragically. I've done all my growing up without him. He meanwhile has stayed the same, the same age. He has never changed.

My father died young, out of season. Just as the good are said to die young. I am middle-aged, a woman of strong appetites and desires, furiously alive; a woman with a tongue in her head. At my age, I no longer live under virtue's shadow. Now I have only myself to praise or blame.

Did he run or was he chased? What raced with him to the final spot, shattering in white retinal glare? That young man in me, the other one who grieves?

When I was younger he never spoke so directly.
When he was younger I never spoke so directly.

Do moths know heaven drawn to a flame?

My father died young and I was surprised. I thought all these years had buried him, that maybe I'd outgrown him, redeemed him, knowing what I know, twice the boy in the woman, the woman in the boy.

3. City of Heaven

I take pains to letter the streets. Grid made rigorous in all directions. Sky locked. Exits clearly marked. Lines ruled. Feet pointing the right way, never up. Streets crossed. Traffic light. Statues armed or at least labeled. Populace populous. Decorous youth prowling in grief-stricken black. Middle-aged adults utterly filled to the brim and thus of no use to anyone. Floorwalkers guarded. Streetwalkers spectacular. Police menacing or impossible to find. Parks geometric and park walker numbers rise exponential to the day's heat peaking at full noon. Radios rocket. Managers on ladders fight their descent on the food chain. Everyone else cut off, cut out to fit or lose.

In the long run, there is no such thing as balance. You are all the way in or you are out of bounds. There is no way to extinguish this dialectic except through draft after draft of textual ethics, the mechanics and clanking machinery of reader-focused phonetics. I feel transparent. As fast as light. Paradise, where there are innumerable back doors,and nothing to be afraid of. Nothing broken. Nothing fixed about it. Clarity in a blink of an eye.

body language

for Thomas

he sees what others do not see. He marries a blind woman who
cannot contradict what he says he sees. He what others do not see
and is often silent about it. He sees the enemy. He sees that there
aren't as many friends as others believe. He sees that he is often the
only person paying attention. He has always been observant and
comes from a long line of observant people.

For instance:

Lip licking (pace)

Eye twitching (arrhythmia)

Crotch touching (impatience, reassurance)

Arm holding (angle of repose)

Neck bent to one side (degree)

Chin lowering (impulse control)

Chin holding (fixed)

Chin rubbing (heat)

Leg crossing (closed circuit)

Leg shaking (tempo)

Knee rubbing (wish)

Ankle rubbing (erase)

Ankle rotating (ignition)

Leaning forward (edge search)

Bottom shifting (agreement/disagreement)

Underpants snapping (punctuation)

Sitting up straight (alarm)

Sloughing (archaeology)

Leaning forward (edge search)

Hip holding (measure)

Hip akimbo (skeptical)

Hip dipping (stroll for the people)

Neck rolling (enemy chasing camouflage)

Hands between legs protectively as one sleeps
Holding oneself as if wounded, holding the side, the position of the
shoulder, the heart, the upper chest, the forehead or the ear
Arms folded across the chest, across the stomach, hands folded
in the lap; fists open or closed. Hands manicured, nails bitten, or
blackened, or veined. Gardening hands, sewing hands, carpenter's
hands, mechanic's hands, musician's hands.
The mouth pursed, folded, pouted, pursed, puckered, projected,
twisted, curled, smirked, smiling, frozen.
The eyes—a multi-vocal choreography—averted, crossed, at half
mast, glazed, in quick darting motion, penetrating, blinking,
unblinking.
Also uncharted, in the dozens, tongue flicking, lap dusting, erect,
stretched, waddling, lengthening, compact.

a day and
its approximates

Reader we were meet to meet

and not disappear in the dredging
the edited ledgers omit antiphonal groans

Reader, you were meant to be legible
even in the failure to communicate
your will to resist snatching defeat from
the jaws of easy victory the truth slips in as a figure of speech.

Reader step into my room
this page faces you . . .
what will I miss if you blink
what blots the ink pens and hems the imagination
what hides in the brackish
back stories hostile to the wobbled word,
what resists being pinned to the truth?

Reader, we are carbon, and more
the exact degree of life is inestimable—
some of us chew ice and others suck chalk
some crave salt before there is savor
others can never be too full of sugar or bourbon
sucker punched and stunned by death's pugnacious brawl
into dream time and song, extending both ends
night into day.

Touch, reader, we were meant to touch
to exchange definitions and feed the pulse of
language. I promise if you step in
it will propel you, me, it:
topple distinctions
ease doubt and belief, and
all that in between.

fool for love

I cannot claim rigor or
music:
blindfold or
hormone heated
hunger

I cannot claim ache—my
bulb dimmed or exhausted
the binary phantom has stopped breathing
calamity in my direction

I cannot claim mistaken
destiny or a hole in the cards
of singularity
a dull solitaire never wins or loses

I cannot claim habit haunts
an empty chair or
drives me to disestablished
echo

I cannot claim arousal
by flame sputter
fire-drowned in
crackle

I cannot claim amnesia
that abandoned plastic bag-
bursting testimonies by the curb
discarded with damp coffee grinds

I cannot claim perfect enthusiasm—
I grit my risk against
high drama yet flowers appear
eye to eye

I cannot claim my grain
is porous and thunder
ready to soak in less heaven
and more earth a ton of mud

I cannot claim my double
won't appear when I least expect her
throwing a tantrum and galoshes
following her thumb
prints. She blows things
out of proportion and she
doesn't always use her name.

If not for the comma

would we be able to call
out pause, before you
and if not for commas
would there be periods after every
word
one constipated thought no ripening but forever
young and finally stuck to our
stubborn apostrophes
toilet paper clinging to the soles of our shoes
creatures of dogma's smug
bracket—

There would be no praise of tumble, no advance of askew
no well placed but accidental pedal
Evening walks would slow to a crawl
who would get out of bed or out of chains,
out of the classroom, out of motionless circumstance
who would let phrase after phrase fall, ever
if not for the reliability of pull
we would never stand up but mark an X
for all the unmarked spots, whether
they met the conditions for *a* or *e* or *I* or *you*

If not for the attraction of cymbals to brass
we would look into silence and think we were
making a sound. We could not have
borne the first and permanent exile
where words summoned our original dreams
which now repose beatless, breathless, trampled
abandoned prematurely yet
legible in the lines and specks, jumps
an unvoiced black and slim and black

and jaunty, and black and curvy, coded
in rhythm, sacred musics stacked in rubble
residue and root, vine and verge
womb, texture and remembered array. As if
never complete, an incomplete space
of where the insistent din meets now.

This is no time for nail biting

even the stones are tired of war
though neutral on the subject of throw weight and carried malice
the audience tries to pry themselves out of the script
because they want to belong to themselves, whatever that means,
but now, its almost time for the news. Gabriel
just to show his muscle is yelling in a reedy tenor
about his favorite program preempted for breaking events
and yes, the reception is sharp and palpable
even if it induces nausea, familiarity, the words,
recognizably impaled, plates of gummy platitude
served in modern translation
there is no end to the supply of wretch or
pity pulled out of the pocket on a chain
read by a newsreader in an even tone. Wasn't he in the 19th century?
Maybe. The atomic age was followed by
the ironic age followed by the screen age, and so
help us through the simulacrum of
whosoevers severed ever between
knowledge and obligation, love's amputation, the last thing
that comes to mind as the end of summer staggers
from one lacerating storm to the next, all
side eyes and unconcealed contempt.

from a Handbook of Quarrels

how what they say about you makes it
say itself through you
its
                    thought bubbles overheard
close captioned in your voice
inserted like a chip in the back of your head
                    the king is dead and long live
Elvis impersonators
        they're the only ones who receive royalties now
quoting the original tenants
and leaving empty suits to writhe on stage
booty bump and drop to feed hungry beats ripping

harmless in a televised cage, there is no
danger here, any more, they got all the signifiers they
need—Nigger is a household
word, domesticated by suicide ideation officers who
look just like you. Today, they are out looking for the
color struck and the color stuck hue by hue,
dead or alive, color drained and poured back into

"Speech enacts domination becoming the vehicle
through which social structure is reinstated.
Speech constitutes its address at the moment of
its utterance." The words puncture
skin in friendly fire, and so familiar it deafens—

Is the speaker the puppet or the puppeteer?
Sleight of hand, an ancient forgery,
conducted in language so under the skin we think
we are speaking our own thoughts?
At the end of the line is that a noose or question mark?

This is where love comes in

for Daphne Lindsay

you are the second light, that can never say
you are the 4th star, the sun is all over you
you are cartwheel, come down to earth please;
you are breeze and beach, the sand in sandwich;
water in your ears, you cup the sound of the ocean in a shell,
you are skip and hop, hoping shape, beyond
scrape, even in twirling you stop yourself before
falling backwards into the mirror, the land that lies
behind you who can say where it begins or ends.

you were the beginning of her
who is she, the figure to be remembered
who is she, you are her shadow from
the ground up, you are there, reading and
waiting for, you are there waiting to be
capsized into she, to pour one pronoun
into another, into the urgent world, the
waiting world of shoe polishing, hair straightening
tongue lashing, into the urgent world, you need
a compass to be sure its you, the her
within you, the her inside in
and you, her outside out,
the urgent world with its pushing and shoving
and disputations
its claim of disinterest, its insistence on continuity
you replacing I and she replacing me,
proves two lines do meet
first as parallels then as rings
like a water drop's merge into a
body of water resembles an orbit
an expanding drop

Octavio Paz's calendar

the sun pours into pools of heat
the same sun you round up to 584 days
I tab at 365 and change not keeping score
traveling the gusts sweeping the sphere
we breathe the same air
eyes open or closed still connect dots
linking one stutter to the next stutter and
another year of stagger to skip to
skipped beat and trick another year's draw
snatched from the jaws of ambiguity.

Not everyone makes it
To face forward towards the sun
Not everyone lives to jump the clock or
outwit the gaze that would turn us into stones
Not everyone lives to wake the dead if they have to.

Time Slips
Right Before
the Eyes

The Massacre of Rocks

1]
Then
when I was loving intemperate,
loving freely loving
inventing

Love for its first time,
I took no oaths as seriously as
I took imagination
to penetrate fog

Raising sight to a person
to help me invent myself more—
in the future—
a scarlet reception.

Enthusiastic.
Guilt free.
Musical.

I wanted love to look like me
from the inside out.
I wanted to look more like me
by looking outside.

I wanted to remind myself to look.
I reminded myself constantly of how I looked
and looked for constant reminders.
A love that needed no naming no further

description; I was its author,
its primary reader—
name, no need of reminding—
I called and I answered.

This love without measure
was constantly measured
measuring all
I imagined

hard body, soft
body, sharp face
chin stubble,
chin tickling, wrinkled,

smiling or frowning
a love of extreme insinuation
unreined the brains' desire
to be loved for itself,

loving one's beloved thought—
hearing it answer yes—
even as the eyes of the beloved are
fixed overhead.

The discovery of love:
an original climaxing phantom
embered
in random sensory touch.

Thermals blanket the skin for the night of attainability.
I loved the melodies in elbows and knees
collapsing on the bed, breaking the seals on the bottle
spilling the long sought magic beans.

2]
In too deep
Even at the brink
the steep is almost always an accident;
playing at the edge intoxicates.

Precisely emphatic.
"to be interrogated" empathy or
centrifugal motion varies the flow of blood
from old wounds to new pleasures

the way one can grow to like
licking the radiant raises the temperature—
from the dry—
re-numbered scale from clitoris to heart.

This is a work of falling apart.
This is a piece of work.
This is the hollow left by reorganized weather,
quotes, looking away.

To love being tied to love,
to re-tie the knots,
to love re-tying the knots.
To love or not to be.

To love being braced for the worst
and the worst arriving just as anticipated
in a white van with expired plates.
To love love's knocks and bruises

Tin pan alley contusions, balladic
abuses, suspense and Vaseline coated lens
—indemnify the past's
regrets the reign of blue, its spectrum of undying love.

The price of love of loving like that.
King of love.
Queen of love.
Royalty of love.

Love's enormous inescapable grip.
Only a noose could be so tight.

3)

Fluent

Baby and bath water have come to an agreement.
Rain has made this easy.
Time gets the details in order—
Clear in the morning, followed by a mix of sun and clouds such as
when you stick to the subject, the verbs appear to disobey but follow
thought's arrow, partner to the breeze. Then love becomes not a
destination but a close reading.

Mood Librarian—a poem in koan

1]
there is nothing like you in the world
and I have lost my page
looking up into your face

2]
the sun sprints across the year
and who has time for sleep?

3]
Every beat has been measured for aches
even as we met we vowed never to overspend,
walking briskly, pulling each other by the hand

4]
I learn from the past
of others' mistakes.

5]
which to choose from
a barely polite calm
or a politic rage

6]
you'll always guess what's happening
counting the same way
wrong

7]
this era is overdue
for writing to leave room for more

8]
un'dizzy me
captain of my ocean
level with a gaze

9]
play
your hand

10]
open up
restless brick
and swallow

11]
the sun situates itself
visible no matter
splashy curve in the umbrella

12]
a new painting of the Duke
calmly boarding Noah's ark
even before the animals have a heads up

13]
catch the ball and now
I throw it

14]
thought in the arc
of the reminded

15]
awake in all directions
leaking container

16]
birds purpose the air
as you purpose
pen and paper

17]
number the formula
for un-worded feeling

18]
the coast is clear
the lines rise up

19]
waiting to be worded
careful

20]
silent body
clean misleads us

21]
my house and there's nobody in it
hey hey
my house and there's nobody in it
hey

22]
fit time to place
even the middle
by itself

23]
stay with the shakiness
until the next thing comes

24]
verbs everywhere
except in this language

25]
we don't vote our dreams
they come after us

26]
after "ecstasy"
laundry

27]
this way
up

28]
things changing into
what they are

29]
nothing so manages me
like my own fears

30]
blue sky broken into legend
what can be done
an irregular sense

31]
all morning to get there
and then in an agitated state

32]
wake up after a fashion
to ordinary collapse

33]
dreams fall under the freight
stricken dull

34]
Dream falls face down
canvas side down
stripped of their letters

35]
words cutting both ways
not just for comparison

36]
but to fly into the sun
and come back a paradox

37]
make a date with a box
who it looks good with

38]
"the sun pours through the window
but I won't let a drop touch me"

39]
quantity
no disgrace in less than perfect

40]
all this light does
put time in the shade

41]
exactly my size
the version in the mirror appears
closer

42]
thinking of
one self
oneself

43]
holding the other hand
prisoner

44]
who are you to me
toe to toe

45]
give yourself an out
where fates summon you

46]
Personality waiting
performed, not created

47]
gaze comes from the top down
squares the body

48]
noisy ice
as the mind races

49]
the body spends itself
exhausted material
an idea

50]
words perform a miracle and resuscitate the body
animate it towards its tasks

51]
the box is turned over
so the body can tap dance

52]
wake the stone

53]
talking as if the bell swallowed
the sun's shine

54]
no record is complete
still interested in the subject

55]
broken glass subsumed into
the bottle

56]
choices made in the dark
in light upon reflection
no heaven

57]
life a
dash between dates

58]
and for a moment
a moment

59]
before sickness tea
after sickness tea

60)
when the notes or words
overlap—poetry

Time Slips Right Before the Eyes

The past is imperfect; it is unfinished.

STORY
She said, "Did I ever tell you this story?"

a story that tells and forgets,
told to me by a loved one who forgets
who she tells, or that
what she tells
she told me before
before she forgot
in time, worried
she might forget
over time
who she loves
who won't forget
who she loves
one moment to the next

Chapter 1: Home

Girlhood. Calamity.
She was born in East Harlem, New York shortly after her parents moved, again, this time from Boston. She was the *first* in her family to be born in a hospital, not at home.

Rinsed off, lotioned and brushed up, a bright-shirted baby, clothes make the pose appearing like a small adult; upright, rigid, a baby in a christening dress; held in place by an infant rack of decorum.

In her light-colored, bright clothes, she remembers being chased through Harlem by children shouting "Monkey! Monkey!" behind her down the street.

Buzz of citied life, tricks of narrative join sections of fixed actions to the next action.

She stayed indoors, practicing the rented piano.

The house ticked with heat. The sun was always lower in the sky this time of year. The sun is not the main character but provides enough light so the teller can remember properly.

Her mother surprised her by announcing that they would soon go on a trip by boat, just she and her Mama, while Papa stayed behind. They would visit her great big family on the island back home.

Chapter 2: (Back) Home

The calamity
Back-home there is a great big family, a yard full of cousins,
"pickneys" and aunts and their husbands, chickens, and horses. A
fancy horse drawn buggy, a *cabriolet*, a large house framed by half
pillars, a broad veranda, an imposing manse surrounded by smaller
one and two room houses. Everyone is related or not unrelated.

She tells one story that leads to another story, one she doesn't mean
to tell. How does she keep the stories apart, from falling into one
another, abandoning her typical discipline, with the anger wrung
out? Her stories appear out of school.

The biggest surprise of all is she has an older sister! who is just the
perfect age for an older sister with pearly gold skin the color of a
peeled banana, with hair the color of straw. The two sisters fall into
talk immediately and they talk through the small hours of the night.

But before she was awake, her ma left and didn't return the next day
or for many days after that; didn't return for two years after that.
Mama leaves without saying goodbye, no goodbye at all, departing
in the small hours, reversing the journey BACK HOME by foot, then
cart, then boat back to New York, back to Harlem and far away
from the miraculously large family, in the green terraced hillside,
a yard full of cousins, "pickneys" and aunts and their husbands,
chickens, and horses. A fancy horse drawn buggy, a cabriolet, a large
house framed by half pillars, a broad veranda, an imposing manse
surrounded by smaller one and two room houses.

The edges of the tale flatten here under the matter of fact; they pin
her in place where she is always a motherless child. Motherless so
that no one sees her; motherless and just always out of sight; so

motherless; she almost loses connection between that old world and the present.

The two sisters grow into one another, become home to one another, even among the proliferating list of responsibilities, duty, duty, and duty of family and household, school, thick as weeds. As the years pass, the older of the two becomes a young woman and men of all ages, some old enough to be her father, arrive at the doorstep, navigating the narrowest of passages.

Duties infiltrate the story, the story has a gender. ALWAYS. Reticence forms a natural wall that becomes a lifelong habit of demarcations, an obedience tied to common sense (uncommon nonsense, it's unspoken twin)) where no one must go.

Chapter 3: An Old Home

Grandfather was a very old man when ma brought her back to the
old home and left her there with her sister.
He was so old he remembered life as a slave.

She remembered her grandfather telling her about how he and his
mother had lived as slaves, and about how his mother was left the
property—the house belonged to two English mistresses and the
steep hills terraced into narrow dirt rows running down limestone
cliffs above the sea had been a tea plantation.

Once, while she was climbing one of the lanes that hugged the
hillside, a cousin atop a horse came trotting upon her in the opposite
direction.

Rather than slowing down, he prompted the horse in a gallop
towards her. In her panic she jumped to brace herself against the
high side of the hilly lane to escape the enormous beast and its
mount as they thundered past. When she told the aunts and their
husbands about what had happened, they laughed and told her it
was just her imagination.

*She begins to unravel the cloth dishtowel she holds, un-telling it at
always the same point in the story. They didn't believe her. She picks
at the thread that binds the selvage of the towel, picks the thread
out of the embroidery, unweaves its close linen and undoes dots and
dashes of its spaces.*

Chapter 4: Going Home

And maybe it was not just her imagination.

Grandfather died, and the house was filled with grief and performance. The main room of the house was so large it had often served as a meeting hall, now was transformed into a stage filled with mourners and a parade of moldy guests.

The guests arrived looking as if they had stepped out of pictures of themselves mourning.

Where had they come from?

They came because they were hungry. A little girl, she was deployed to join the ranks of the other young females, a supporting cast of servers to ferry chicken and boiled green bananas and breadfruit and stew and rice and peas and fruitcake and punch and rum and then more chicken and stew and irish potatoes and rice and yams and punch to the guests.

They came to hear tell it. Stories, as Pat said, are repeated to someone who wasn't involved, to get your side of the story told. To be repeated until the target of the tale is clear.

They came to count up the dead, to assign a number, to assess the house, the property, the holdings, the unmarried, the number of sisters, the aunts and their husbands, and the cousins, legitimate and out of wedlock, and the space left in the family cemetery amid the bush and tamarind trees.

Her ma came back too, at the end, when the guests had thinned and they had already laid the old man in the ground. Mama came with one full suitcase and an empty one. She'd been waiting for her.

She never stopped waiting. The mind on its
own continues to count days she was left
with her grandparents, changing every time
she tells the story or untells it. Was it 3 years
or 5 years? She was 4 when she left New
York; 7 years old when she returned.

Like trying to get the corpse to stand up
straight. The dead come and go as they
please. She stops in memory's tracks to get
her bearing.

The past is far from perfect. It is unfinished.

A woman is painting her own body. She is painting herself from her
own perspective, to have that kind of self-possession.

First, she uses spirit lines to diagram how the Spirit runs through her
in every direction.

Then she is drawing and recording the excess
of the body where parts are illegible.

Then she is recording the absent parts, where
the body has been worn down, trails into
dribbles on the map.

Like trying to get the corpse to stand up
straight.
These unfiltered dialogs with the dead who
make an order where they stand and
come and go as they please.

She stops in memory's tracks trying to get

*her bearing. Mama had this photo made
to remember her daughter by. When I turn
it over the back is full as well 102 years
margin to margin.*

(for Daphne Lindsay 1918)

Lineage

Where did they come from?
Bleeding down to her antecedents. Written in block letter
Work with the clutter of the un recollected.
It never crossed their mind. No one travels between worlds like they
used to.

It seems every generation had been trying to fly with varied success.
It seems that for every trapeze, some jump. Some did scissor kick.
Some did bridge two points the old world and the next. Some did
balance on sand. Some did drop from a complicated scaffold. Some
did tumble. Some did escape. Some gave in on arms and knees
praying to stop the fall.

The Awful Truth

Each day challenged to make sense
and (the type of cents that beget sense)—folding money—
short cut walking against traffic,
on a retraceable path,
bend coincidences neatly in half—
cause and effect;

Each day tip of the hat, hold my lap ready to fill
my filled-up lap, crawl around sleep deprived
fight off boredom
hold my tongue
using my other hand
to hold off boredom
exercise patience
dismiss the random thought
a fly on the shoulder
wish for acres of free time
the thirty-second day dream
avoid incoherence and become
coherent, consoled, able
taking the long view.

Each day to look for beauty
read something that escapes the blind spot
come round the bend, read the whisper
content outside the left margin
over and above creature comforts
unspoken questions on the buffet line of
rationed happiness, who is A and who is B and
who is L and who is able? And why G and why
R and why W and how to grow? How does sun
spot, rain cloud, tides fall, dreams speak?

For Fern

Come, let us play the memory game
in the never told, where the dead live
in the "before you were born"
when all the interesting stuff happened,
in the unopened
toy bin, where the better toys lived,
in a book that had a door
you could feel the draft in letters
at the bottom of a drawer beneath unworn lingerie
in lines you wrote down but forgot
they were written by you
about someone else
about the future: Remember
when we knew
how to be old and a bit hard of hearing?
the best of friends walking
on a cold night across the park?
This world would be forgotten if not for us (a hill, a valley,
a red road connects the two by weaving in and out of green pastures
Brahmin cows heat dazed on their knees under the yoke of the sun).

A cistern so deep it went well over to the other
side of the world, we were cautioned to never go too close
lest even our voices accidentally vault the edge
and never be recovered, muffled
until the end of who she say what.

They fixed a wire net over the top to
break the fall so no one tests the net,
no dive to rescue doused body, no message lost on a child

but loaded and time delayed as adult gaps in speech, and
good diction to hold the unintended spill—
just breathlessness and
open eyed dark water
roaring lessons in
keeping the room
fit for company.

Should You Find Me

Should you find me, I'm the short one on the left, knocking brown against green hills, a fleck in the crowd, not be blinked on or peeled, coming off with the tape.

Should you find me, would you have a word for me, or do I go forward on faith for a new word, different spelling.

Where would you find me? At the top of residential grids, in the tear downs and the private cul de sacs, or at the bottom, in the nameless streets, pavement dwellers tapping into the futility lines for brown out power?

Where would you find me? Which kidnap do you mean, you ask? In security chambers, handcuffed, soundless zeroes maximum cancellations of futurity? In the malls' maw thrall of fear numbing card bearing youth? Or in abandoned villages smoking ruins patrolled by uzi besotted soldiers? When the codes change, does the energy suck remain the same?

Would I recognize my name in the voice calling from the burning bush? Would I hold my breath and hope it wasn't me, and if it isn't me who else will carry the tune?

If you should find me, would I have to relearn my own name, talk to the letters in the alphabet, one by one, my new best friends? Would I have to invent spill over: there's got to be more days in the year, birthdays shouldn't be rationed, we need new shoes, we need to replace perpetual war footing?

If you should find me, does that mean the pop quiz in the picture-rebus times pantomime tariffs pygmy? Would I button down? Do fewer wrinkles in the forehead automatically lead to new wrinkles in the knees?

If you should find me, could I stop doing, doing, doing red onions, beets, radishes, peppers? Then who would restore the color to crunch? Everyone knows it's not easy to hold things still: the red and its expectation, the bell and its clapper, the beet to its sugar.

Should you find me, how could I miss? Who would I miss? Who would miss me?

If you should find me, I would measure as it has taken time to learn how, practice a long view: the pinch, a pause, punctuation in the moment.

love's

An accident that detains you. You've come all this way and the road breaks down into branches, the way lost. Car parts litter the road, force descent into the breakdown lane. You lift your head as if there is something to see coming toward you at the scene of the accident, but there is nothing, nothing to see but piano silences to break through the patches. Nothing but your number, facing up in the broken traceries of your pal. Nothing but the middle between you and your destination.

But nothing is as it seems. Smoke or zeroes mix. All this way to have dropped the key or the ball missed the boat or the point. All that splashy show of omnipotence only to have the remote grabbed from your hands and the button set on unstoppable independent motion. All that dread frozen in place.

Is it dread that keeps you from waking or moving out of the way? The train, the truck, the ambulance picks up speed, headed your way, flashing light, pedestrians scattered. The flash catches you within its frame, a pinhead in its sights. You look in the mirror a long time, trying to reconstruct the look of surprise that formed there, but catch instead the line of jaw you seemed to have inherited from family, a trick of age, one face supplants another, a formula opening, as in "once upon a time," and you appear, only older.

First note, last note, the same And when you finally awake, you have not missed a beat.

With toys of fortune we try our hands in time, win or lose. We throw ourselves into the rhythm of he wager, an easy game of back and forth. The dice tumble contained within the paradoxical limit of win or lose, no matter the stakes, the same. The house always wins.

But oh how burnt carbon tastes across the lips. *Love is*. An exquisite dance for fools. We dare each other to fall

Into each other's arms. We practice and pretend to spin, even bounce over the speed bumps to savor provisional suspension.

Veronica:
A Suite
in X Parts

veer iconic

into the sucking pools of lost recordings, that veer iconic beyond
moan
where there is nothing to count on, question, quote
in pre-arranged territories that eliminate safe harbor, but break
thought, limits
grief, barely marks massacres, multiplies brutal lack. . . .

"Someone matching your description"

you wake me up, Veronica
to escort you to the door to the unknown
I am slapped awake and paperless;
my eyeglasses abandoned on the ledge
startled
a tongue triggered dry
staring into eyes emptied of the exact shape of
mercy. they are ice.

you, Veronica, are beside yourself
your face a burned down house
count
me in so I can walk with you, Veronica
though you are mostly alone

(even)
dry eyed
at your own funeral

(even)
being of two minds is not enough
when Jacob
wrestled with an angel
I wonder
who wrestles with me
or you (even)
to argue "reasonable" doubt
when I know they never leave their
guns
they carry them
in churches, bars and court rooms and put
"scare" quotes around the world

they
are never mistaken
there are no words for mistake
no words
for mistake
no reason for indefinite register

they speak in a prose that refuses to be tamed by thought's inflection,
always mad as hornets in a front pocket, inedible, stuck on the fear
of deserved reprisal, the axe that never quite falls, hold that thread
please, so they call to quarry, prey, foot stool and chattel, someone's
back to stand on, to enable them to climb the ladder faster, unletter
the ladder faster and limit equality to a single call, a single meaning,
a single tongue, a simple song for how long.

there are no words
for mistake
no
obvious thread that binds the master
to the missing supply of mastery

(even)
sleeping history's abolished fictions
live absent the bigot
whose afterthought is our
undermine

(just)
one knowing: what is known from before
and knowing what the owners of copious knowing

know
without speaking, say without saying

exactly, "be my scapegoat, my sex toy, my
just dessert, my bowl of candy
profits, my penciled thought, my extinction."

Ghost Names

Veronica whose ghost name is
    Vida, wept to be a grandmother at 35
    for don't stones desire to be touched?

Veronica whose ghost name was
    Yvette, who other girls lay in wait to fight her
    everyday,
    bitten by one fierce girl
    while other girls laughed so out of body,
    they never noticed the bites scarring their own bituminous
    skin.

Veronica whose ghost name was
    Evelyn, was murdered by her husband
    for even a rock wants to dance,
    and not to be hurled and broken,
    orphaning their children and children's children.

Veronica whose ghost name was
    Henrietta, brought from Antigua
    at 16 to warm a stone of a man almost three times her age
    outlived him and her seven children.

Veronica whose ghost name is
    Martha, whose rage at martyrdom,
    turned her arms into resting missiles
    all knew never to cross.

The heart
moves from one side to the other catastrophe
or gets hit in the forehead

or shoved (always out of nowhere) pulled by
the reins of female obedience, killing us.

V sticks out like a battered peace sign
V as in what victory?
Like parted legs.
 an unexpected sharp corner

Veronica

how we got here we don't know
Veronica with her weird dandelion socks
me, fresh from the whirl wind, the bulls
eye, the twirling pinwheel—
one hand over my heart

but the matter facted this in cement
we were in narrow straits

how straitened? how narrow?

(doorknob be my heart!
heart be my door!)

we were out of key
and out of connotation
the eviction notice said as much
we were out of sweet talk
no words for the straits we were in
chilly hands picked my pockets
no cool, no sangfroid to blanket froth

nothing but a truth—burned to the ground

we were in narrowed straits
how narrow, how straitened?

could it have been his tone of voice?
the question itself is illegal
heart-on-the-sleeve?
everyone knows that's bad for business

no business dreaming—
that's a quote
you know you're not supposed to sleep during the day
it will make you ineligible
for the wheel of fortune guest pass and citizen zombie benefits

Bad intentions? Intentions
can stroke or bruise while supplies last
Shit happens or so they say
mostly to the uninsured mothers of gunshot teenagers

We were in narrow straits, Veronica
suddenly surrounded one
by the dozen
people turning around facing the wind.

We were out of fine points
when you're a hammer everything's a nail
we were out of patience—
no one could miss the obvious coming

We'd always paid attention (what price, what loss?)
but randomly assigned names. For instance, someone
mistook Veronica for me, as if our names were
interchangeable syllabically, for Black, female,
fat, thin, poetic, shy and angry, unpredictably
angry, closets filled with mysterious *anger*
coming from nowhere to erupt
anywhere

car park Kmart mall campus bedroom bathroom stall doctor's office
emergency room prison
one size fits all
hanging in the brackish melon-hibiscus-chlorine scented

calm of public space—a bright red fuse
waiting for reliable unreliable weather—

Veronica and I are unreliable weather
with mismatched closets of rage
potentially the mothers of gunshot teenagers
prone to brine
and fixed turbulence despite the sieving motion
in history, the retrieval of balance between reason
and perspective does not apply to us, instead
we teeter on the brink of boiling vertigo.

Nerves strain thin in narrowed straits
How strait, how narrow?

The man with the largest gun boasted he was still standing
the trial went on for years
you could lose his face in a crowd
we forgot our hands over our hearts
did not grow there, almost forgot how we got here

the man with the largest gun keeps on talking
issuing statements through his lawyer
this trial could go on for years
with our hands over our mouths.
We were out of excuses
day after day the bodies pile up
friends with the wrong police

how did we get here, we used to know

spark—can you speak in rain?
question—do grave stones mark free?
rage—can you escape cage death while chained to necessity?

We were in narrowed straits
how straitened, how narrow?

We were out of science—
it suited closed eyes.
We were outside of temperature
I passed out brown paper care bags to
the fellaheen, street weary foragers
breaking their fast out of the skeleton dumpsters

no luck with sixes, sevens
or even elevens, Veronica claimed
my pockets spawn zeroes and
we were ready to turn on
each other the fire hose of free floating ire
but for this—

we exchanged our hands over our hearts
hers for mine and mine for hers

Suspicious activity

"Forty three percent of the people killed were not in the middle of committing a crime but were stopped for 'suspicious activity'"

A resting face.
She abandoned the cloud
and chose to go out on foot.
She was missing
a grin.
She knocked at the wrong intersection.
He defeated a match
stick.
He crossed di-
agonals.

They moved past
an uncovered spot.
They lost pump.
He was bowing in erratic directions.
She ran by spurious gloat.

They were potential trouble
makers—did not fit
the turn down-dressing of
the neighbor
hood who was speaking
in concealed carry
He bolted out cork dizzy
thinking free from the lockdown

She traced the body
that refused to fit a
grammar of disappearances.

She studied how Black
people getting excited in a
manner different than others
drives some people to
blunt displays of panic
and violence.

She studied how Black
people getting elected in a
manner broader than others
drives some people to
blunt displays of panic
and violence.

Lamenting in an
appropriate structure has
rendered her hoarse from
not screaming.

She is blind from reading
from inside her lids.
I would show you where it
happened on a map, but
the cursor of the public's
attention has vanished.

Upon another acquittal
(a choreography of grief)

for Mamie Till, Sybrina Fulton, Samira Rice and Geneva Reed Veal

She hd neded to heal but
She had promised

Her blues angled-slipped out
capsized
travelled a long distance

under water
the sun casts a blurry silence

& looking
refused border, filled her mouth with scorch
& when I saw her

fall into herself
(not her first grief)
& crumple in an instant
knowing no justice will ever be found
could be found

where nothing is said out loud
& when it is said or wailed

the something said is
something that no one hears:
everything will be taken from you
even more than you know will be

taken
—away

& it will sever you
make you swerve—

stagger
as if punched in the heart
or in a part
you can't easily name

talked over
punched into
so you pivot, as if possible
to get out of the way

I write as if words'll
suspend your fall

gentle you
when there is no
de
parting agony

Mourning Birds

Here a thousand birds dispute[5]
The gun going off
the random back fire
who handled who
and who rose to be recognized
and how the body came to be fresh
fallen there
and why the girl was tackled
and how her wrists looked slight in hand cuffs
and the exact nature of the orange pin
and the load glassing her eyes
the load incalculable and
the incalculable load

Here a thousand birds dispute
the fresh blood on the sidewalk
the battle line, how it was drawn
how the sides were chosen
had there been a trial
Or any doubt and if so
how it was framed
did the shot hang in the air and who
was there to hear it, and here
Hold this thought—4 are shot per day

As xenon follows its element
Or night its day time shadow
As penumbra fades into solids

5 After Paul Éluard "here a thousand magpies dispute"

and endures a rain of blows
—there falls a reign of blows

Here a thousand birds dispute
What went wrong
the stopped clock
the orange pin
the random call

the fall from childhood
the fall, the incalculable fall,
the fall incalculable

this time to not let the familiar
obsequies mask obscenity
twist lips, the birds dispute

these too, the televised worship of cinders is riveting
junk heartache abetted by hollow gestures

The birds' disputations grow louder
frantic against glass
stunned splintered and hushed,
in shadowy, honeyed innocence

The gun going off
The random back fire. . . .
appears as random as asking
who's got the gun
who owns the gun
who sold the gun
who pulls the gun
and who does the gun let sleep?

After a dream deferred

(We waited. Apostrophes in our tool kits
Ready to take possession of ourselves.)

We got to doing what we thought needed to be done and we did do
what we needed to at the time to become the people who did what
needed to be done.

Scanning the skies
To put a period to a history of
Our undoing
The other whom they think they know
(as if the spirit can be caged)
or postponed

I wait to be young again, Veronica
And it may be too late now to reverse
Blues-deep tangle around the ankles

I long to take off these boots, don't you
And plant my feet in a common direction,
And part my fingers to better
Feel the pour of the invisible air.

Soft Assault

(for Cauleen Smith)

If thought balloons'
undetonated rage blooms between
the one and the other "public,"
trained to duck-
walk around them
then walk into me, as if
I loom transparent, tendering
Blackness symptom-like
broken glass marring "public safety:"
unpoliced
disproportionate reaction:
a bullet for every wallet
a hail of bullets for every call
for help triggers.

I walk the through and through
clamor of unblinking red
living blurred surviving
the received phrase book
substituting the actual
for the literal
by any means   soaring
by any means ecstatic
by any means hanging
by the tips of my wit
by any means with a nod to the joke
by any means detecting the risible in the visible
by any means punching the line
by any means scotch the litmus test
by any means reining in the stutter

by any measure give gravity one more try and stop
the clairvoyance of
soft assault for each step
one takes in public.

My heart is armed and loaded.
A rage blooms within me.
A garden of ragged breath. The facts
are bone breaking. The first shovel in
looks a lot like the last shove in
my grave.

Body Double

What you need to know about this:
sometimes I am that body looking for trouble.
I find myself looking the way I behave the way I am suspected
fingering the scarves, gloves, the flamboyant
ly priced straight jacket
not even my style and doesn't suit me
but irresistible because I
could be sticky
and according to legend
light fingered from moment to moment:

Cancel the gavel of contempt
and the constant enforcement of weeping!

Sometimes perception is the jail that fills in the facts

the body and its image
returns "value" more than words
can harm you—
the image of a man beaten
beaten broken bloody
body put on re-beat
sets the metronome in back
brain to static—amygdalic crack attacks
metallic jaws set to imminent
threat addiction; a life put on stall
filmed to repeat edged in flames
drowning mind in its almost
death without dying
but poison set pressure
sky high to die

it rains on us daily
breaking the body in breaking news
a broken record
re-beats our re-beaten hearts—

I am wrapped
in inscrutability
surrounded by volumes
thick with ink
of what they think
but don't know
I am that arrow drawn against
the machine of sure extinction

Heat seeking
Heart seeking
Broken hearted
Half hearted
hurt

I want to drain the mechanics of
innocence which has never been a defense
obedience in three shades of violation
and indignity.
(they are losing)
because my collective noun is untying the knot
(they are losing)
because my collective noun is fighting gravity
(they are losing)
because my collective noun is fighting the box with a ring
jumping the gun.

what could go wrong?

There's no bruise like one I'm going to get
It grows large in the imagination
a shiner running rings around any bruise you've ever seen it's
stupendous it's yugely calamitous a calamity like you've never seen it
runs rings around any catastrophe in the car crashing est Hollywood
movie you ain't seen nothing yet like this collapse collapsing on you
the waters break the steam rises and a hot rain pours down
rain that makes the rivers boil you ain't seen boiling until you've
seen this this is the noise set to pause us

unless we make it ourselves it is immobilizing
when I want noise to shuffle
my pre-conceived
bed to tomb surnames
nearly illegible and worn
where will that noise be coming from?

we have to ask or risk parting with the ringing of heart beat or
eyelids flutter into smoke

where is that noise coming from? we spew into flutes to gain air and
a sense of where the trail may have tapered off tune, breaking into
forest and trees, when mostly they are hardly distinguishable in my
calm I understand now how my bones pop upon waking, they are
tuning up to temperature they are tempo and laissez faire as long as
they stick to the spine, curved in a perpetual hunch over the glowing
hotbed of the screen.

No one knows where the noise comes from that sometimes we
mistake for ourselves speaking.

Broken English

(Lamentation)

Wound up in words
wounded
re-wounded
the beaten
bulleted body
repeats
wound
reads
into ache
stead
y
or not
ready
RED
already
or not
b/red
read
b/roken
syllab
les de
tachm
ent.

It's
not better
remember
red
It ren

ders
s
peechle
ss
tend
ernes;
it
strip
s
kin
dred
lik
e
ki
ndling
i/nto

bro
ken states
rende
rrra-ra-ring
ileg
ible
and unintel
l
igible
wher
e
blac
kness sup
presse
d-d-d-d by laws
severed
tongu
ess

to co
wer
us, and s/cowl
us de
ad
mute.

Yet she (I)
to speak
all at once
the thing
that has been on
her (my)
mind
which words
(verbs)
reco
ver
dignity?

restores
let
letters to the unm
uffled
(unmuzzl(ed))
full
-throated-sound as in
some-bodied?

the dead
lines (t)each
the proper order of time
scorch (ed)
zones of property,

propriety's
(in) tension
returns me
days after day
to variations of question:
how to breathe
freely
despite shackle-rattle and
pummeled jolts? Where does glare
recede?
when do words lead
to care
beyond site
and out of sight
a path to better resist?

On occasion, we produce history, the present's surprise

We measure speed by the absence of interruption.
We measure safety by the string of near misses.
We anticipate the end by who is telling the story.
At this time of night, there is a machine that calls you by name and talks to other machines where you live, where you dance by your fingertips over the globe, an address at a time, day into night.

This machine feigns a reckless intimacy with you, corrects your spelling errors, as if reading your mind, but skips over others, like replacing eros with errors and spiraling with spelling.

The other machines are being dismantled. They tell a different story. They draw the attention of the curious, the ones willing to go out of their way—past the land of leaves drop, the valley of forgetting, over a bridge too far, past the flag of fictitious victory over to the corner of vanquished subjects, where uncommon love is almost concealed.

Sorrow Songs

*To self-immunize against provocation, she says every morning, "the
devil won't win
today!"*

Bills due show the cost of
fatal forgetting if we break speed traps
~~If we stroll topsy they see turvy~~
If we tell tell we become consequence,
If the truth comes out, they still think we
're exaggerating.

Gravity lands
predictably. G force ropes us into place
if you watch carefully, even jumps are tethered.
We who oppose—
(Who is this we?)
Against our worst nightmares
we grow brighter in the dim fact of
our condition, "not to study the monster
and forget to study the monstrosity"
its persistence.

if you blink you might miss us
If you are always in the light of power
you would think is there a mote
a moth
an after thought
humming in the static
death march of counting
what matters

Nowhere means every place
is already taken
to be curved or conditionally stopped
at the place you're at
where you are snapped into place
positioned and jelled into a line of extinction
A certainly orderly decease amidst the mayhem.
Don't interrupt.
They got you.
I get you.
You have been gotten.
You dangle from a possessive
case, a case of possession.
One coordinate shift to the
right or to the left will slide you off the map
leaving an echo where once you were a blinking light,
a persistence.

It will be great
I mean, we will be great.
I mean, we will finally know greatness. Not wandering around in a
sea of compromises. Enough to make your eyes cross while keeping
tabs on your pile of troubles to make sure it doesn't grow
much larger than the next fellow's—just pull back just so

Look out: the sea is restless
and the ice is melting, and the ice keeps melting
past the data points scrubbed from websites,

The ice has melted beyond paper,
gone from ice to water,
to air, to dry, to voiceless.

The blues they say spills
from one broken heart to the next
An open measure

falling into the spell of itself.
The head is a homing device
the feet follow.

The work of the map is to exaggerate home
The work of the body cannot
be proclaimed enough

The fact that the body moves
while also being a home stacks the odds to our credit,

water breaks inside the body
flowing from cell to cell
but it does not slake thirst.

I swim in air
towards home that can no longer
be found on the most meticulous of maps
but must be found by north's irresistible tug and roar
without it I would be lost.

Instructions for Waking

1. Recall how many steps in a comb In the critical mass of hair and part,
2. Refer to surge of papers in the undergrowth? Wake up and watch
3. the houses lean, generationally, the voices gale
4. expand in the force of grace, from the edges of the room
5. Listen for the chords the radio brooms
6. over dreams lately gone. Tune finger after finger,
7. morning's indexical count. Recall the wind that gets us on our feet.
8. Before samba there was salsa before salsa there was zouk,
9. before zouk there was mbalax, before mbalax there was bougaloo
10. the motion takes over the sound track, the dead leaves rise up and bow.

Instructions for the next chapter

1. Look out, but don't mistake it for forward.
2. Look outside yourself, against recognition
3. will you notice when the streets are given over to rain?
4. It is difficult to wage speech in the heat of battle.
5. Running the risk of being insufficiently multiply inclined.
6. Lies tend to accumulate around supposed truths.
7. What is there left to believe?
8. They will plead rank even as they empty their guns.
9. Take us off the cross.
10. Ride the glory of suspended narrative
11. Glory of paint applied thickly.
12. There's more there than you have been led to believe.

Instructions for travel over land
(pandemic version)

1. The boom comes from the sound
2. Tracks into the grave
3. Opening the ground beneath the feet
4. The window opens into an abyss, and no
5. net appears. There are no wrong doors, at least none
6. we will acknowledge.
7. But sharp knocks and
8. Steps triplet and legato
9. The crowds are patient and stately at the exits
10. Windmill signal fly off blur
11. Vanish into tunnels
12. the underworld cracked open
13. And we survived by inserting ourselves between pulmonary thumps

Context is all

This me, not that me, that them, no, the other them, that we, or this we, all we, both of them, and all of we, when there, not here, but me then, before then, and before we, when we, how we, when we spoke then, never spoke back to them, then. Silent we, resilient we, existed, as an existential us, observing with restraint and bemusement (terror), a noisy them, childish them, and if we over-spoke, we spoke using our bodies to them, head tilted or hand back at them, or facing them with all our backs, never breaking face, so masked to all senses of them, all tenses of we, over-prepared.

We had better. We had better be better than them. We had better be better beginning and end, early and fitful. We had better be better beginning and in the middle, too. Be better between life and death, better in the visible and sure better than them in the places they overlooked, than them and their soundtrack. We had better be better than them who draft and re-draft them-selves, "what destroyed me, created them," or so we thought mistaking the well off for well-being, enough to be them, so some of us thought an thought better of. We had better be better being draft selves than them even if it meant drowning in virtuous poison.

Fr**dom

ignites in me plenitude
that scents rain. Sense
the sky is full of surprising
music. Timpani, trumpet

a blue tent torn that orders
cogent, cumulative event in which no false intonation
claims itself king

over all. Every last woman
man, and child proof the rain falls
never to be worn out

Freedom is the breaking point beyond rage
I'm not scared and I don't care where the dream
undertakers have warned me not
to take too much, not to
love too much, not to look too closely at the past,
What could there be left to break?

Nothing left to be broken
Nothing left to be taken.

This is where love comes in

there's so much to do for justice, we're running out of brink. so
I grab my socks and pull them up. slip the latch on my one-track
mind and avoid the chair that catches me with a nap. I point my feet
in the left direction, prove, I am all ears, work with the pivot, the hip
the city, its dance map, avoid the cemetery of stubborn spots. avoid
walks with a slow crawl, and notice the furnished detours along the
way

Each step one takes in public, jars the partially apprehended
panorama of the cookie cutter's regrets and is an occasion to
learn from the field of the interior. Here—the street home, catalog,
collected histories of first aid and relief, post no bills on dread, seek
out uncollectibles, be suspicious of fancier goods lost then found,
bravery starts from the bottom love notes warriors send souvenirs
home

The simple assault of questions too numerous to canal, the sky's not
the limit, it turns out the breeze a whisper of eighth notes detached
from the staff, birds wing by named and numbered in regimented
flight, no words without commitment to the act of answering
or defaulting to an I don't know

This is where love comes in coat on or coat off, hat on or hat off, go
back for gloves, go back for umbrella, go back for scarf, for plastic
orange glasses, rain boots with frog face on the toes, Both the kids
like them, their small hands fit perfectlyinto mine, let few events
escape; they mark every page like a book mark or as if joy dropped
on the path a few days ago will show up later in melting snow

The back of the future

The future is back
so where do I begin
The future is back and it is
ungovernable
It's back and it sucks
Just as I've been told
It's all in the hands
the future's back
and it's been frozen in place
a germ, waiting to thaw
The future's back and x marks the spot
where it was last seen
picking cotton, cutting cane
The future's back and can't remember what it came into the room for
The future's back having locked the keys in the car
The future's back no gimmick, I promise.
You're the prize
YOU
The future's back and swim is what we do next
The future's back
a dance craze
The future's back and they've loaded the clocks with slugs
The future's back and the light is imperfect
The future's back—crawl into this
The future's back and I don't see our names
(Fill in the curves)
The future's back in a disjointed q and a
The future's back: first time farce
second time tragedy
third time ecological collapse

The future's back if you go far enough
The future's back take it from here
The future's back to perfect the art of dying
This time. Again.
The future's back
time on strike
The future's back under an assumed name
The future's back—what have you done for me lately
The future's back we read the introduction this time
The future is back and the story leads you here

Lines on Love's (Loss)

for Ahmaud Arbery, George Floyd, and Breonna Taylor

what we do not dream we cannot manufacture

Art follows ear and echo
covers/chooses
selective
eyesight searches the dust
and is surprised by love's
apophatic blinking

what love sees in daily light
holds open color – ink, roar, melody and quiet
is its own steady gaze
to better endure bumps

"always more song to be sung" between the words
jars memory and its subatomic _____
moving at the speed of thought _____

in random thirsts rise_____
naming the sensations, _____
fishing for breath, _____
combing through hair as tangled as nets, as_____

thick as the beat of blossoms' _____

a fine line between mind and senses spinning _____
in which her/my/their body becomes expert_____
without waiting for unified theory,
loving the body of one's choice and _____

to live so surrounded _____
with fewer asterisks and _____
more verbs and _____
less security alerts _____

there eloquence before _____
and above
_____the grave.

Wavering: adios, vamos, scat

If every goodbye is a rehearsal . . .
their paradise is where the end stops

and that would be shredding, flagging, staggering
and that would be strolling, hovering, stunning
and that would be heaving, healing, divining

standing under correction's bright light
the sun sets without dissolve
the horse careens riderless,
body tossed in one direction

the soul in another episode's
plot by number funeral or flowery
we "customers" of the apocalypse
stumble into the upswept zoom of flirt and tumble

into confession's temptation to succumb
face to the game. no bystanding—
bruised toes never stop repeating
an exclamation, heart—
felt all over the planet.

(pandemic version)

AUTHOR'S NOTE & ACKNOWLEDGMENTS

It is difficult
to get the news from poems
yet. . . . people . . . die miserably every day
for lack
of what is found there.

    —WILLIAM CARLOS WILLIAMS

Read again that archeological sentence,
that syntax that determines a cursus planus"

    —JAY WRIGHT

What time is it?
(on cross-beat: three against two)

    In 2020, a year that will be marked as a portal or an abyss or both, reading these poems strikes me as a lens into a poetics of the present. Whether the poems are in lines or in blocks, fragmented, or in "cursus planus" a plane/plain course, they come across as objects I made as I listened to my own or others' expressive/digressive linguistic peregrinations through the world.

    As a history of the present, a poem is an immanent artifact, language in action written in dialog at a specific time, multi-sided, cubed and layered with the writer's circumstances. A poem has an afterlife of its own, hits a pitch resonating with the past imperfect, askew/aligned with the present time.

    In these poems I re-collect the old Cold War, as well as the continuous present wars of domination; I mark the struggles for Black Freedom, women's, and queer liberation, as well as the backlash, and suppression that violently animate our present.

Some of these poems abstract swift eddies of personal history: places, causes, family—tangents and intention, preoccupation and purpose. Poetry as wager as Joan Retallack says, and as survival, as Audre Lorde reminds us, these poems were and are a rehearsal space for emancipated knowing, thinking and feeling; the open space of hope that through invention and play, lies a road to getting free.

I'm grateful to the publishers who brought versions of these poems to print in earlier books. I've tried here to be thorough, any omission is unintentional; I am sustained by multiple communities of poets and writers, named and unnamed here.

Versions of these poems appeared in *Local History* (Roof Books), *Arcade* (Kelsey Street Press), *Piece Logic* (Carolina Wren Press), *A Day and Its Approximates* (CHAX), *Time Slips Right Before Your Eyes* (Belladonna* Collaborative), and *Veronica: A Suite in X Parts* (selva oscura press).

Thank you to the publishers who saw these poems into print: James Sherry, Patricia Dienstfrey, Rena Rosenwasser, Charles Alexander, David Kellogg, Rachel Levitsky and Belladonna* Collaborative supporting innovative writing by women, and Fred Moten and Kenneth Taylor. For shepherding the present volume through an unpredictable 2020, I am grateful to Katy Lederer and Nightboat Books's Stephen Motika and Lindsey Boldt. Readers complete the text. I am grateful to Tonya Foster, John Keene, and Yanyi for their rich and collegial readings of my work.

Poems have also appeared in *BOMB, Boundary 2, Cave Canem: A Gathering of Poets, The Brooklyn Rail, Best American Poetry, MEANING, PEN America, Hambone, Fence, Nocturnes,* and *Mixed Blood.*

Thanks also to poet interlocutors over time in workshops at Poetry Project, Cave Canem, Furious Flower, and Naropa. Thanks to the artists whose work has inspired and graced my books: Alison Saar, Lorna Simpson, and Carmen Hererra.

Abiding thanks to these friends: Charles Bernstein, Adam Fitzgerald, Tonya Foster, Adjua Greaves, Dawn Lundy Martin, Tracie Morris, Julie Patton, and Simone White.

And for all that is constant, in whose generative care I grow bolder and fueled with love: Marty, Madeleine, Julian, and Jon.

ABOUT THE AUTHOR

Erica Hunt is a poet, and essayist, whose works include *Local History, Arcade, Piece Logic, Time Flies Right Before Your Eyes, A Day and Its Approximates,* and *Veronica.* Her poems and essays have appeared in *BOMB, Boundary 2, The Brooklyn Rail, Conjunctions, The Los Angeles Review of Books, Poetics Journal, Tripwire, Recluse, In the American Tree,* and *Conjunctions.* With poet and scholar Dawn Lundy Martin, Hunt is co-editor of an anthology of new writing by Black women, *Letters to the Future,* from Kore Press. Hunt has received awards from the Foundation for Contemporary Art, the Fund for Poetry, and the Djerassi Foundation and is a past fellow of Duke University/University of Capetown Program in Public Policy. Currently, she is a Bonderman Visiting Assistant Professor in the Literary Arts Program at Brown University.

NIGHTBOAT BOOKS

Nightboat Books, a nonprofit organization, seeks to develop audiences for writers whose work resists convention and transcends boundaries. We publish books rich with poignancy, intelligence, and risk. Please visit nightboat.org to learn about our titles and how you can support our future publications.

The following individuals have supported the publication of this book. We thank them for their generosity and commitment to the mission of Nightboat Books:

Kazim Ali
Anonymous
Jean C. Ballantyne
Photios Giovanis
Amanda Greenberger
Elizabeth Motika
Benjamin Taylor
Peter Waldor
Jerrie Whitfield & Richard Motika

In addition, this book has been made possible, in part, by grants from the National Endowment for the Arts, the New York City Department of Cultural Affairs in partnership with the City Council, and the New York State Council on the Arts Literature Program.